kl

To my

Joe

Pappy

In the Workers' Interest:
A History of the Ohio AFL-CIO, 1958-1998

Warren Van Tine
C. J. Slanicka
Sandra Jordan
Michael Pierce

1998

Center for Labor Research
The Ohio State University
Columbus, Ohio

Library of Congress Catalog Card Number: 98-86957

ISBN 0-9666284-0-3

Printed by
Typographic Printing Company

CONTENTS

FOREWORD

A newspaper reporter recently asked me whether "labor is back?" I could have answered with my own question: "Back from where?"

The real answer is that the Ohio AFL-CIO never went away. Since 1958 we've always been here — caught, it seems in recent years, in the same struggles that shaped our beginnings and will stay with us as long as there remain selfish forces in society attempting to deny working people their dignity and rights.

But that answer wouldn't have satisfied the reporter. He was more interested in whether labor was back in "power."

As we celebrate our 40th anniversary, it's difficult not to admit that we are feeling our oats, just a little bit. The Ohio AFL-CIO was a central figure in the defeat of an anti-family workers' compensation law in 1997 and we were involved in the defeat of a sales tax scam in May 1998.

We saw both issues as an attack on working families. It's fair to say that during my forty-three years in the labor movement, any small sense of power we might feel comes from battles fought in the interest of all workers. And that sense of power stems from the understanding that our victories are impossible without the grassroots support of union men and women courageous enough to enter a fight that benefits not just them, but all working families.

Those trade unionists are in the background of virtually every page of this wonderful history of the Ohio AFL-CIO.

In the Workers' Interest chronicles some remarkable achievements by leaders I was fortunate enough to have watched from my earliest days in the labor movement. They taught lessons that remain with me to this day. Who would have guessed, for example, that at the height of price gouging by auto insurance companies, the Ohio AFL-CIO would have offered a low-cost alternative after losing a legislative battle seeking to control insurance rates.

In one sense, we were powerless to stop the forces of greed that resulted in exorbitant car insurance rates. On the other hand, we had the creative energy and power to offer an alternative. Our venture into that nether world of commerce was short-lived, but at least it was an attempt to offer a solution in the best interest of workers.

Without that creative energy, labor never would have stopped the right-to-work coalition that helped speed the merger in 1958 of the Ohio State Federation of Labor and Ohio CIO. And without the power generated by grassroots union members, we would not have won that fight at the ballot box. We were up against a well-organized, well-financed foe — a foe that had the support of the state's major newspapers and its major industries.

Sounds familiar, doesn't it? The Ohio AFL-CIO stood up against virtually the same foes when it decided to challenge a regressive workers' compensation bill at the ballot box in 1997. We were down in the polls, we were outgunned financially, and we were opposed by the major industries, the major newspapers, and the party controlling the Statehouse. And after years of counting on, but not consulting with, our grassroots, we weren't real certain they would still support us.

Well, we proved that the Ohio AFL-CIO is back —

back because the source of our power never went away. Trade unionists young and old joined a true David vs. Goliath fight, and once again David was the victor.

That grassroots power marks the beginning and the end of this first forty years of the Ohio AFL-CIO. The authors of *In the Workers' Interest* have done a masterful job linking together the middle years, the history that has shaped this organization.

As our history shows, we won some battles and lost some. Times have changed and more change certainly awaits us. But the need for our existence will not change and the struggle "in the workers' interest" will remain.

These first forty years have been a long and tumultuous journey, but in a sense, the authors allow us to understand that we've never been away.

William A. Burga
President, Ohio AFL-CIO

INTRODUCTION

In late September 1998 over one thousand union members from across Ohio will gather in Cleveland for the Ohio AFL-CIO's Twenty-first Biennial Convention. At the gathering delegates will elect officers for the next four years, pass resolutions establishing the organization's policies, and cheer politicians vigorously campaigning for election in November. A few moments will also be taken to commemorate the fortieth anniversary of the Federation's founding in 1958. Only a handful of those in attendance will be able to claim having been present at the creation. A few others will be able to trace their involvement back to the early 1960s, including President Bill Burga who was a youthful delegate to the second convention. A majority of the delegates in 1998, however, will be of a generation that has come of age since 1980.

We have written *In the Workers' Interest,* first and foremost, to remind older unionists and to inform younger ones of the heritage of which they are a part. We are also hopeful that this book will lead a wider audience to understand more fully one of the most influential organizations in Ohio and some of the historical events and issues it has helped shape. Last, but far from least, we hope that the academic community will find much of merit in these pages. There is a dearth of scholarship on state labor federations since the merger of the American Federation of Labor and the Congress of Industrial Organizations in 1955. In filling this void, a study of the Ohio AFL-CIO is particularly valuable because of the importance of the state in terms of its industrial development, size of union membership, and prominence in national political affairs. Moreover, as the following pages will reveal, the Ohio AFL-CIO led the way among state federations in its political action program, its efforts to inform and empower the rank-and-file, its fight on health and safety issues, and its extensive involvement in community services. While we have shunned formal citations in the interest of economy and readability, we have provided a note on sources at the end of the volume to highlight materials upon which we have drawn and to guide future researchers.

All praise — and likewise all blame — for what appears below goes to the four authors, two historians and two labor educators, each of whom is deeply committed to the labor movement. It was our decision as to what to include and what to leave out, what interpretation to give to various developments, and for establishing factual accuracy. Other individuals possessing other values tackling this same project would inevitably have produced a different book.

Still, we would like to recognize a number of people for their help in this endeavor. The officers and staff of the Ohio AFL-CIO have been unhesitating in providing us with any records we have asked for. We would like to thank President William Burga and Secretary-Treasurer Donald Day for taking time from their busy schedules for extensive interviews. Since the mid-1970s the Ohio AFL-CIO has been turning its records over to the Ohio Historical Society for public access. All of the staff of the archives, but particularly Bill Myers and Gary Arnold, were invaluable in helping us use this material. Our appreciation also goes to historians William Childs, Russ Coil, and David Stebenne for their encouragement and assistance. All these individuals and organizations, in their own ways, made this a better book than it would otherwise have been.

March, 1998

Warren Van Tine
C.J. Slanicka
Sandra Jordan
Michael Pierce

Chapter One

Triumphant Beginnings, 1958

I

Wednesday, May 7, 1958, turned out to be a very pleasant Spring day in downtown Cleveland. The night before the temperature had dropped to the low 40s, but under sunny skies it had already climbed into the 50s by 9:30 in the morning. At that hour, well over 2,000 delegates, alternates, and spectators started filling Cleveland's Public Auditorium for what promised to be a momentous development in Ohio labor history. While they sat around in little clusters waiting for the day's program to begin, some discussed the strengths and weaknesses of the Cleveland Indians, whose record stood at 10-10, and whose roster included such legends as Rocky Colavito, Herb Score, Hoyt Wilhelm, and Larry Doby. Elsewhere in the hall the conversation focused on which was the better car to buy, a six-passenger Dodge Sedan for $2,088, or the $1,789 Nash Rambler, which could be paid for in weekly installments of $9.25. Delegates who had spent the previous night at the movies exchanged opinions on the performances of Montgomery Cliff, Elizabeth Taylor, and Eva Marie Saint in *Raintree County*, or Clark Gable and Doris Day in *Teacher's Pet*.

Less talkative were those who paid the ninety cents general admission to see Brigitte Bardot in the "adults only" showing of . . . *and God created woman.*

Certainly these topics seem old-fashion today, but in 1958 they were not merely "quaint." The delegates making their way into the Public Auditorium possessed values and attitudes forged by their experiences during the Great Depression, World War II, and the Korean Conflict. John Glenn had yet to orbit the earth; Bill Clinton had just become a teenager; and Michael Jordan was not even born. Still ahead lay Kennedy and Johnson, the Great Society and Vietnam, Nixon and Watergate, Carter, Reagan, and Newt Gingrich. A glance around the auditorium revealed the predominance of white males in the labor movement as in most public arenas of American society. With the Civil Rights Movement still in its infancy and the Women's Liberation Movement not yet started, not surprisingly only about 100 of the 2,300 delegates at the convention were women and even fewer were African-American. The working-class delegates in attendance, however, dressed in classic 1950s middle-class style — dark suits, white shirts and ties for the men, and frilly dresses and, in some cases, hats for the women. No knit shirts and blue jeans were in sight. And equally noticeable as the clothing was the cigar and cigarette smoke filling the air, causing both the official convention photographer and those from the press to want to take as many pictures as possible before the developing cloud became too thick.

Despite these visible differences from today, several commonalties connect the past with the present. Those delegates quietly awaiting the session by reading the *Cleveland Plain Dealer* saw stories with a markedly modern ring. One story discussed angry protesters throwing rocks at Vice President Richard Nixon during his trip to Latin America. Another item focused on the seemingly constant rain in the southern part of the state which was causing the Ohio River to approach flood stage around Cincinnati. The sports page featured news that Middletown High School basketball star Jerry Lucas would play college ball for Ohio State. Much of that day's newspaper coverage, however, was devoted to the primary elections held the day before. On the Republican side, William O'Neill won renomination for Governor, as did John Bricker for U.S. Senator. Michael DiSalle would again be the Democratic challenger for Governor (having lost to O'Neill in 1956) and Stephen Young would try for the Senate. The paper also reported the grim news of the continuing recession gripping Ohio. Since May 1956, factory employment in Ohio had dropped by one-sixth — or a total of 228,000 jobs. Few sectors of the economy seemed immune from the downturn, but the steel centers of Youngstown, Warren, and Canton experienced the worst effects as employment dropped twenty-three percent. Indeed, for the gathering delegates the substance of the last two newspaper stories — politics and jobs — provided the reason for their being in Cleveland on that particular morning.

As ten o'clock approached the delegates broke up their discussions and headed for their assigned chairs. Then, precisely on the hour, the youthful Ray Ross, President of the Ohio CIO Council, and the elderly Michael J. Lyden, President of the Ohio State Federation of Labor, jointly sounded a gavel that steelworkers had forged the night before at the Kaiser Aluminum plant in Louisville, Ohio. The first constitution convention of the merged Ohio AFL-CIO came to order.

II

The two organizations that merged that spring day brought with them contrasting heritages. The Ohio State Federation of Labor was by far the older of the two bodies, tracing its lineage back to June 24, 1884. On that day, labor representatives from around the state met at Union Hall (20 E. Main Street) in Columbus and founded the Ohio State Trades and Labor Assembly. Influenced by the politically-oriented Knights of Labor — at that time the dominant labor organization in the nation — the Assembly's primary mission was to lobby the state Legislature on such issues as establishing the eight-hour day in state contracts, abolishing convict labor at the Ohio Penitentiary, and restricting child labor. Thus the predecessor of Ohio State Federation of Labor was already on the scene when the American Federation of Labor (AFL) was founded on December 10, 1886, in Druid Hall in Columbus. While various leaders of the state organization helped establish the AFL, the Assembly continued to maintain an independent existence, working with affiliates from both Knights of Labor and AFL. In 1897, the Assembly formally joined the AFL and changed its name to Ohio State Federation of Labor.

Over the next half-century, the fortunes of the Ohio State Federation ebbed and flowed with the state's political climate. The Federation's greatest accomplishments occurred between 1910 and 1914 when it worked in tandem with Democratic State Senator William Green — who was also a district officer of the United Mine Workers and who would go on to be President of the AFL from 1924 to 1952. During this Progressive era, the General Assembly passed the state's pioneering Workmen's Compensation Program and established the

Industrial Commission to set safety rules and provide arbitration and mediation services. For most of its existence, however, the Ohio State Federation of Labor shied away from political action. In harmony with national AFL President Samuel Gompers, it feared that efforts to use legislation to advance labor standards — such as minimum wage and maximum hour laws — could be twisted by the more powerful business lobbyists into legislation that actually tightened restrictions on workers. Rather than subject their interests to the visitudes of politics, the Ohio State Federation of Labor reasoned that workers should rely on their economic muscle and win gains through union contracts. When the Ohio State Federation did engage in political activity, it usually sought laws creating a fair collective bargaining environment by prohibiting injunctions in labor disputes and banning the importation of strike breakers. Thus, the Federation was not exceptionally assertive during the New Deal era of reform in the 1930s and did not systematically start to mobilize its membership as voters until after the United States Congress passed the anti-labor Taft-Hartley law in 1947.

The Ohio CIO Council, in contrast, had emerged as part of the massive unionizing surge of the 1930s. For years the AFL — composed largely of skilled craft workers — hesitated to organize the mass production industries despite the rapidly growing number of Americans working in such factories. During the depressed 1930s, however, industrial workers, encouraged by favorable federal legislation, most notably the National Labor Relations Act (or Wagner Act), took it upon themselves to launch their own organizing drives. They received active support from such prominent labor leaders as John L. Lewis of the United Mine Workers

(UMW) and Sidney Hillman of the Amalgamated Clothing Workers of America (ACWA). In October 1935, after the AFL convention in Atlantic City proved unwilling to strengthen the Federation's commitment to mass production workers, Lewis, Hillman, and several other leaders launched the Committee on Industrial Organization to do the work. The leadership of the AFL expelled the UMW, ACWA, and the other unions associated with the organizing committee, leading the group to transform itself into the Congress of Industrial Organizations (CIO) in November 1938.

Ohio was a major playing field both in the CIO's efforts to unionize heavy industry and in the rivalry between the AFL and CIO. Many members of the Ohio State Federation of Labor, however, actively supported the CIO drives among rubber workers in Akron, steelworkers in Youngstown, and autoworkers in Toledo. After the divisive 1935 Atlantic City convention of the AFL, the Ohio State Federation still sought some middle ground and seated delegates from the rebel UMW and United Rubber Workers at its 1936 state convention and furnished speakers to some CIO rallies. Such cooperation and the CIO's increased success in Ohio raised the ire of the AFL executive board, leading it to demand that city and state central bodies terminate ties with CIO affiliates. No longer able to participate in Ohio State Federation of Labor affairs, in February 1938, representatives from forty-eight CIO unions, as well as fifteen CIO city and county labor bodies, established the Ohio CIO Council as a political lobby of their own. The next decade-and-a-half witnessed full-scale competition between AFL and CIO unions for members and contracts and intense animosities between leaders in both camps. At the local level, however, there were also numerous acts of cooperation.

From its beginnings the Ohio CIO Council was far more political than the Ohio State Federation of Labor. Early in its existence, the newly-formed Ohio CIO Council established the Ohio Labor's Non-Partisan League to mobilize voters behind pro-labor candidates in the November 1938 election. Indeed, John L. Lewis and other CIO leaders insisted on organizing mass production workers not only to strengthen labor's economic muscle but also to give it meaningful political clout. The concentrated strength of rubber workers in Akron or steelworkers in Canton and Warren could influence the state's political process far more than various skilled craft workers scattered around Ohio.

Eventual reconciliation of the two competing labor groups occurred slowly and was pushed on them largely by external events. America's entrance into World War II following the Japanese attack on Pearl Harbor on December 7, 1941, dictated the need for more cooperation from all segments of society. Thus, representatives of the AFL and CIO at the local, state, and national levels found themselves seated together on an array of committees designed to mobilize materials and morale to win the war. The growing conservative, anti-union climate of the post-war period, highlighted by the passage of the Taft-Hartley Act in 1947, fostered further cooperation by the two groups.

Events in November 1952, however, proved pivotal in bringing the house of labor back under one roof. Within a span of twelve days, both William Green, President of the AFL for nearly thirty years, and Philip Murray, President of the CIO since 1940, died unexpectedly. Their passing dealt a harsh blow to the American labor movement since it confronted both the AFL and

CIO with the difficult task of choosing new leaders who could meet the pressing problems of the 1950s. At the same time, though, handing over responsibility to men who had not played major roles in the original split provided a unique opportunity to terminate the old quarrel. The Republican victory in the November 1952 national elections dashed all hopes for the repeal of the Taft-Hartley Act and mandated an end to the divisions among labor.

Both Walter Reuther, the new head of the CIO, and George Meany, the new President of the AFL, saw labor unity as essential and sought to settle the differences between the two bodies. Consequently, in June 1953, they concluded a no-raiding agreement among the constituent unions of the two organizations. Union piracy and jurisdictional strikes had long been a disruptive force within labor ranks and perhaps the greatest continuing obstacle to reunification. Advancement on this front allowed next for the establishment of a Joint Unity Committee, headed by the two new presidents. The committee kept its deliberations secret, so that few outsiders knew what progress the committee might be making. Thus, with great drama the committee announced on February 9, 1955, that a merger agreement had been reached. Meany and Reuther told reporters that in the new AFL-CIO each affiliated international union would preserve its identity, the no-raiding agreement would continue, and the special departments within the old AFL would remain, to be supplemented by a new Industrial Union Department for CIO affiliates. As befitted the party to the merger with by far the larger membership and treasury, the AFL obtained both the presidency — George Meany — and the secretary-treasurership — William Schnitzler — while Walter

Reuther became Vice-President in charge of the Industrial Union Department.

III

At the formal merger convention of the national AFL-CIO in early December 1955, President Meany expressed his wish to see all state and local bodies united by the end of 1957. Yet that was not to be. In the more unionized and industrial states, particularly those in which the CIO had the larger membership, negotiations proceeded at a snail's pace. In Ohio, except for a February 1956 "get acquainted" luncheon for the top leadership of the two state bodies, nothing else happened until April 1, 1957, when George Meany wrote Phil Hannah, Secretary-Treasurer of the Ohio State Federation, urging action. Several factors accounted for the delay. For one, the leadership of both organizations had lots of other issues to occupy their energies. Then, too, there was concern about the division of power and offices within the new organization, particularly since in Ohio — unlike nationally — the CIO was by far the more powerful force. And finally, the Ohio building trades unions resisted any merger before the leadership settled thorny jurisdictional issues.

Yet, no matter what the excuses for the delay, there were also compelling reasons for establishing a united labor movement in the state. In 1957 the Republicans firmly controlled the General Assembly as well as the governorship, placing organized labor on the defensive. Encouraged by the state's conservative political climate, delegates to the October 1957 convention of the Ohio Chamber of Commerce voted to consider an initiative petition to amend the Ohio Constitution to prohibit the union shop, as allowed under the federal Taft-Hartley Act. While such a "Right-to-Work" amendment would hurt the entire state labor movement, the measure would be particularly harmful to the building trades in the Ohio State Federation of Labor, the most reluctant caucus regarding merger. By 1958 eighteen states had adopted measures to prohibit the union shop, including neighboring Indiana in 1957, the first northern industrial state to do so. Embolden by this victory, right-to-work forces viewed Ohio as ripe for a victory. Like Indiana, Ohio was noted for its conservatism and politically weak labor movement. In 1955 Ohio labor had suffered a two-to-one defeat when it sought to use the initiative process to obtain major reforms in the unemployment compensation system. The Executive Vice-President for the Ohio Chamber of Commerce gleefully reported on this defeat at a subsequent meeting of the U.S. Chamber of Commerce. He then predicted success with a right-to-work initiative since the state's labor movement was divided, union members appeared unresponsive to the movement's leadership, and farmers and other conservative groups could be counted upon to oppose labor's political aims. As Robert Rowe, legislative representative of Ohio Public Employees Council, wrote to Ohio CIO Secretary-Treasurer John Rooney, "Whether or not Right-to-Work appears on the ballot . . . the general political climate and previous lack of intra-Labor cooperation which has made it possible for our enemies to seriously discuss such a proposal have also produced bad laws in general. As a case in point, then, Right to Work should help our people understand the need for greater participation in the labor movement as a whole."

And it did. As August 1957 progressed, Hannah was able to persuade John E. Breidenback, President of the Ohio State Building and Construction Trades Council, that jurisdictional disputes were a national, not a state, issue and should not be grounds for resisting statewide merger. Consequently, at the Ohio State Federation of Labor convention at the end of August, the building trades withdrew two resolutions which would have put the Ohio State Federation on record against unity and instead agreed to let the talks move ahead, although Breidenback declared, "with some reluctance."

In all, the pressure from Meany, the threat from the Ohio Chamber of Commerce of a right-to-work initiative, and the Ohio Building Trades Council's change of heart dramatically speeded up the merger process. On August 20, 1957, the first meeting of the Joint Merger Committee was held, during which it appointed a negotiating team composed of Ohio State Federation of Labor President Michael Lyden, the Federation's Secretary-Treasurer Phil Hannah, Ohio CIO Council President Ray Ross, and that organization's Secretary-Treasurer John Rooney. On January 28, 1958, after eight working sessions, the negotiating team presented to the full Joint Merger Committee an agreement and constitution for the new organization.

The merged state body would initially have a President and an Executive Vice-President, both from the Ohio State Federation of Labor, while the Secretary-Treasurer would come from the Ohio CIO. The Executive Board, however, would represent the actual membership distribution in the state, with the Ohio State Federation of Labor getting only ten members while the Ohio CIO would have fourteen. The Merger Committee well understood that the office of Executive Vice-President was only a temporary arrangement so that seventy-five-year-old Michael Lyden could be honored as the first President of the Ohio AFL-CIO before retiring from a long and fruitful career in the labor movement. On February 14, 1958, George Meany approved the state's merger agreement as consistent with national AFL-CIO policy with only minor revisions requested. The leadership of the Ohio State Federation of Labor and Ohio CIO then made plans to hold a merger convention in early May, during which each organization would first meet separately to approve the arrangement, and then they would come together, united.

The final road toward merger was not without its bumps, however. On the Ohio CIO side, confusion arose when Secretary-Treasurer John Rooney, who was slated for the same post in the merged organization, resigned to take a position with I.W. Abel on the international staff of the Steelworkers. In the end, the Ohio CIO Executive Board agreed that the new post should go to Elmer Cope, thus keeping the secretary-treasurership in the hands of the Steelworkers, the largest union in the state. On the Ohio State Federation of Labor's side, Breidenback and the Ohio Building Trades Council reasserted their opposition to merger because the national Building Trades Convention in December 1957 failed to satisfy jurisdictional concerns. Indeed, when Lyden and Hannah presented the proposed merger agreement to the Ohio State Federation of Labor Executive Board at a January 27, 1958, meeting, it was approved only by a vote of five to two, with Breidenback and Frank Fischer of the Electrical Workers dissenting.

The conflict within the Ohio State Federation of Labor also provided the major moments of drama when the two state bodies met separately on Monday, May 5, to formally accept the merger accord. Despite a reputation for being the younger and more unruly of the two labor organizations, the Ohio CIO's last convention on May 5 and 6 in the Music Hall of the Cleveland Auditorium went off without a hitch as the delegates unanimously approved the merger agreement. At the Ohio State Federation of Labor's convention in the adjoining Ballroom, however, a free-for-all broke out. Feeling that the Federation's leadership was ramming the merger through the convention, about twenty delegates led by Breidenback charged the platform, knocked over the speaker's rostrum, and began swinging their fists. It was mostly a battle of old men, for both Ohio Building Trades Council President Breidenback and Ohio Federation of Labor President Michael Lyden were seventy-five, and Ohio State Federation of Labor Secretary-Treasurer Phil Hannah — whose coat was split from shoulders to the waistline — was fifty-six. When peace was restored, the delegates finally approved the merger by a vote of 810 to 354, with the largest cluster of nays coming from the building trades. The Ohio State Federation of Labor did not meet the next day, but rather Lyden, Hannah, and other leaders circulated around the convention hotels trying to mend fences. In the end, most of the dissenting delegates remained in Cleveland to participate in Wednesday's united gathering. Having shown loyalty to leadership of the Building Trades Council, they now democratically accepted the decision of the Ohio State Federation of Labor's majority. Breidenback, however, paid the price for going beyond the boundaries of fair opposition. Originally slated to be a member of the merged AFL-CIO Executive Board, his name was withdrawn and he drove back to his home in Dayton.

The Ohio AFL-CIO's First Constitutional Convention was clearly a gala affair. At 11:13 am on May 7, 2,274 delegates representing 799 local unions and fifty-five central labor bodies voted as one on merger. Ohio thus became the thirty-seventh state to execute a merger, but it was the largest state yet to do so. As was appropriate on an occasion designed to bring once-warring factions together, the leaders avoided contentious issues and championed resolutions that enjoyed widespread support. Delegates spent most of the convention listening to stirring addresses from such luminaries as Walter Reuther of the United Automobile Workers, I.W. Abel from the Steelworkers, Joseph B. Keenan of the IBEW, and AFL-CIO Secretary-Treasurer William F. Schnitzler. Even the election of officers went smoothly, in part because of pre-convention planning, and in part because the men elected were of unusual merit.

The Ohio AFL-CIO's first President, Michael J. Lyden, was the senior statesman of the state's labor movement. Born in Ireland in 1879, he immigrated to the United States at age nineteen. In 1903, he joined the Amalgamated Association of Street Railway Employees in Youngstown and helped negotiate the local's first contract. In 1910 he became the local's President and served in that position for thirty years. In 1912 he was elected Secretary of the Youngstown Labor Congress, in 1924 he became a Vice-President of the Ohio State Federation of Labor, and in 1935 he began his twenty-three year presidency of the state body. Two attributes made Lyden a fitting first President for the Ohio AFL-CIO. First, he had an honored record as a pioneer labor lobbyist in Ohio, championing such reforms as workmen's compensation and improved public education, which benefited all of working class Ohio regardless of union status. Secondly, unlike many AFL leaders, during the 1930s Lyden actively helped organize industrial as well as craft workers in the Youngstown area. Indeed, he aggressively defended the steelworkers during the bitter "Little Steel" strike of 1937. Such a profile made the "grand old man" of Ohio labor an ideal candidate for pulling the labor movement together.

Executive Vice-President Phil Hannah, who at the second Ohio AFL-CIO convention in 1960 succeeded Lyden as President, also had deep roots in the labor movement. Twenty years Lyden's junior, Hannah had grown up around Scranton, Pennsylvania, where as a youth he worked as a breaker boy in the region's anthracite mines. His life as a miner and UMW member ended abruptly when he was injured in a slate fall. Needing to find other employment, he moved to Cleveland, where he worked as a gas station attendant. His career as a labor leader commenced when he successfully organized the local pump jockeys as part of the International Association of Machinists. By 1958, Hannah had been Secretary-Treasurer of the Ohio State Federation of Labor for sixteen years, although he had taken a two-year leave of absence to serve as Assistant Secretary of Labor for the Truman administration.

Like Lyden and Hannah, Elmer Cope, the new Ohio AFL-CIO Secretary-Treasurer, was a well-known labor Democrat at the time of the merger, although as perhaps befits someone emerging out of the CIO he had a more left-wing political past. Born in Elwood, Indiana, in 1903, Cope went to work in a tin mill in Warren, Ohio, at the age of sixteen and soon joined the Amalgamated Association of Iron, Steel, and Tin Workers. Through both hard work and luck, he earned a bachelor's degree at Swarthmore College. There, Cope fell under the political spell of A.J. Muste and went on to take classes at the famous Brookwood Labor College in 1929-1930. After which, as an organizer for the socialist Conference for Progressive Labor Action, he returned to work and union activities in the Warren area. In 1936 he joined the staff of the Steel Workers Organizing Committee and faced the daunting task of organizing Weirton Steel in West Virginia. During World War II he served as Director of District 27 (Canton) of the United Steelworkers of America (USWA) as well as on the Fifth Regional National War Labor Board. In the post-war era, the CIO sent him as a delegate to the World Federation of Trade Unions in Europe, where in 1949 he led a split to protest against Communist influence that resulted in the founding of the International Confederation of Free Trade Unions. Immediately prior to assuming his duties as Ohio AFL-CIO Secretary-Treasurer, Cope had been Director of Economic and International Affairs for the USWA. Cope brought to his new post a reputation for hard work and determination.

IV

The first task facing the officers after the adjournment of the founding convention was to make the new Federation operational. Neither the Ohio CIO headquarters at 218 E. State Street in Columbus, nor the Ohio State Federation of Labor headquarters at 273 E. State Street were large enough to accommodate the combined staff and operations of the two groups. Thus the first Executive Board meeting decided that temporary operations would be housed at the old CIO office while the Federation's facility was torn down, the adjoining property purchased, and a new, 10,000 square feet structure erected. The entire project was completed within a year, with the new headquarters celebrating with an open house on Monday, November 19, 1959, although formal dedication ceremonies were not held until June of the following year. The attractive brick, two story building, highlighted by an impressive glass mosaic, cost about $200,000 while the land it occupied was appraised at around $120,000.

The new headquarters at 271 E. State Street became home for a highly talented staff which included Gregory Stebbins as Director of Compensation and Safety, Don Smith as Public Relations Director, Ira Thompson as Comptroller, Orville Jones as Education Director, and Jane Adams as head of the Women's Activities Department. Matching the numerical balance in the overall organization, CIO members held a majority of the staff posts. Likewise, the *CIO-News & Views* was simply transformed into the weekly Ohio AFL-CIO *News & Views* and the name given the Ohio CIO's political program, *Common Cause*, now became the title of the merged organization's legislative efforts.

Finally, the new state body faced financial difficulties. It inherited, of course, the accounts of the old Ohio State Federation of Labor and Ohio CIO, so the merged Federation was clearly solvent. However, to make the merger as palatable as possible to affiliated unions, the first convention had set the per capita tax at four cents a month, knowing that was inadequate. The leaders hoped that an increase in affiliations would bail out the organization, but that was not to be, in part because the Ohio AFL-CIO asked only for a modest $2.00 initiation fee to encourage local unions to join. By May 1960 it was apparent to the Ohio AFL-CIO Executive Board that a higher per capita tax was needed, and so a one cent increase was sought at the second convention.

V

When the founding convention adjourned on Friday, May 9, no one present had any doubts about what the first challenge to the new organization would be — defeat the right-to-work initiative in the upcoming November election. In the closing moments of the convention, Phil Hannah warned the delegates "that a wind is rising and the river is flooding. That wind bears bad bodings for our great Movement."

In September 1957 delegates to the Ohio Chamber of Commerce annual meeting had approved a right-to-work initiative campaign, and the following month a front organization, Ohioans for Right-to-Work, was established with Theodore Gray as Executive Director. According to the *Cleveland Press*, however, Herschel Atkinson of the Ohio Chamber of Commerce, Don Wiper of the Ohio Manufacturers Association, Clyde Wallingford of the Ohio Petroleum Manufacturers, and George Hammond of the Ohio State Council of Retail Merchants were the men "huddled in the exclusive Columbus Athletic Club masterminding the campaign." Early in January 1958 Ohioans for Right-to-Work filed with the Secretary of State a proposed amendment to the State Constitution which read: "No employer or labor organization shall deny or abridge the right-to-work by requiring membership or non-membership in, or payment or non-payment of money to, a labor organization as a condition of employment or continued employment in this state." In order for the amendment to appear on the November ballot, Ohioans for Right-to-Work needed to collect some 355,000 signatures from qualified voters. To this end, Ohioans for Right-to-Work spent $250,000 over the next several months, paying college students from such elite schools as Oberlin $18 a day and twenty cents for each signature they obtained. Such firms as Armco Steel, General Electric, Timken Roller Bearing, and Cincinnati Milling contributed the money for this purpose. With these resources, Ohioans for Right-to-Work had little difficulty gaining the needed signatures by early August.

The Ohio labor movement refused to passively accept these developments. In early February 1958 — months before the merger—leaders of the Ohio CIO, the Ohio State Federation of Labor, District 6 of the UMW, and the state divisions of the railroad brotherhoods formed United Organized Labor of Ohio (UOLO) to coordinate efforts to defeat the threatened right-to-work initiative. Since the leaders of the various labor organizations were occupied with other issues, including merger, they recruited Walter L. Davis, Associate Editor of the *Cleveland Citizen* and former President of the American Federation of Television and Radio Artists, to serve as Director of United Organized Labor of Ohio. The steering committee of United Organized Labor of Ohio also made four very critical decisions early on. First, it decided not to fight Ohioans for Right-to-Work's signature-gathering campaign, which most likely would be successful, thus saving United Organized Labor of Ohio resources for the actual ballot contest. Secondly, it concluded that to be able to stop the right-to-work forces it would need to build a broad-based coalition that pulled in groups outside the labor movement. To this end, the steering committee decided, thirdly, to keep the campaign against right-to-work separate from the other political and election activities the Ohio AFL-CIO coordinated through the Committee on Political Education (COPE). This strategy enabled United Organized Labor of Ohio to find allies opposed to right-to-work who might not agree with the rest of labor's political agenda. And finally, learning from the disastrous 1955 unemployment reform initiative, United Organized Labor of Ohio decided to hire professional political consultants to advise it on campaign strategy.

On Labor Day 1958, many political commentators predicted another major setback for unionism in Ohio. So too did the bookies on Cleveland's Short Vincent Street, who even in late October offered seven-to-five odds on a right-to-work victory. Two factors stimulated these negative prognoses: the large amount of cash that Ohioans for Right-to-Work raised for its early-summer signature-campaign and the widespread endorsement of right-to-work by newspapers around the state, who too often interpreted their editorials as reflections of public opinion.

Yet, in reality, momentum in the battle had shifted from the proponents of right-to-work to the opponents. Funds coming into the Committee for Proposal No. 2 — the successor to Ohioans for Right-to-Work created after the signatures were collected—slowed to a trickle. Some potential backers held back donations, convinced by the editorial writers and also, ironically, by the rhetoric of union leaders that the right-to-work forces already had amassed a huge war chest and were well on the road to victory. Other business sympathizers feared sending the Committee for Proposal No. 2 funds after the Court of Appeals in Cuyahoga County ruled on July 29 in the *Cleveland Cliffs Case* that corporate contributions to influence voting on ballot issues violated the Ohio Corrupt Practices Law. In the end, the proponents of right-to-work borrowed heavily from both the Huntington Bank and the Ohio Chamber of Commerce (although the latter loan was really a donation since it was never repaid and written off as a "bad debt").

Along with cash problems, fickle allies plagued the campaign for right-to-work. Many a businessman may have privately supported right-to-work, but shied away from having his firm publicly identified with the effort. Thus, the most visible business backers were also the state's most notorious anti-union companies, like Timken, a fact that helped drive home the true intent of the initiative in many voters' minds. Likewise, until mid-October otherwise sympathetic politicians, fearing voter alienation, at best timidly supported the right-to-work initiative. While the Ohio Democratic Party platform bluntly urged "the people to vote no on Constitutional Amendment Issue No. Two," the more business-oriented Republicans took no stance. Instead they simply encouraged "all citizens to inform themselves of the provision of this proposed amendment and to vote in accordance with their convictions." Indeed, Republican Party leaders had unsuccessfully tried to persuade the Chamber of Commerce not to seek right-to-work during an election year out of fear that the issue would drain funds and votes from its candidates.

While the right-to-work campaign was losing momentum by Labor Day, United Organized Labor of Ohio's drive was building up steam. During the spring and summer, Walter Davis, Elmer Cope, Phil Hannah, Ray Ross, and others had crisscrossed the state helping to establish grassroots organizations in most cities and counties to fight the right-to-work proposal. They also helped amass a war chest with large contributions coming from the UAW, Carpenters, Machinists, Steelworkers, UMW, and the national AFL-CIO. In addition to donating money to the statewide campaign, a number of unions contributed more directly to local efforts. The Teamsters Joint Council 41, for instance, gave $20,000 to the Cleveland Federation of Labor to fight Proposal 2. Equally important, though, were the 1,375 local unions that contributed one dollar per member to defeat right-to-work.

Organizers spent a good portion of the funds on a massive voter registration drive. "Quietly and methodically," the *Akron Beacon-Journal* observed, "the unions got their members to register to vote. This amazing drive produced the biggest crop of eligible voters in history in every urban center except Youngstown." Critical to the successful registration drive — as it would be in the November "get out the vote campaign" — was the work of the Ohio AFL-CIO's Women's Activities Division headed by Jane Adams. In an age when a majority of married women worked at home rather than in the paid labor force, union issues reverberated throughout the household. Consequently, in 1958 Adams recruited over a thousand housewives across the state to laboriously compare union rosters with county voter registration files and then to contact by phone or letter unregistered unionists and explain to them how to sign-up. Volunteer work by women exceeded 120,000 hours; over 300 women each gave more than 100 hours to the campaign.

Also critical to the registration drive was the work of Ohio AFL-CIO staff member Warren Pate and other African-American trade unionists. In a November 1958 report on voter registration, the national AFL-CIO observed that in Ohio "Negro groups working with COPE were particularly effective. Three thousand Negro union members were registered for the first time in

Youngstown, 25,000 in Cleveland. In three hours, 155 Negro unionists were registered in Massillon. Our people canvassed barbershops, beauty parlors, churches, and civic groups in an unprecedented registration 'blitzkrieg'."

Along with a stunningly impressive registration drive, United Organized Labor of Ohio proved extremely successful in building bridges to other constituencies in the state. Widespread African-American opposition to right-to-work was fostered when the Forty-Ninth Annual Convention of the National Association for the Advancement of Colored People (NAACP) went on record against the proposal. In a pamphlet published by the Ohio NAACP's Committee on Political Action, Martin Luther King, Jr. of the Southern Christian Leadership Conference, Roy Wilkins of the NAACP, A. Philip Randolph of the Brotherhood of Sleeping Car Porters, and Lester Granger of the Urban League, all urged Blacks to vote against Proposal 2, declaring that "'Right to Work' promoters are the same people opposing school desegregation in southern states." In a similar vein, Cleveland's African-American newspaper, the *Courier,* editorialized: "We have cast an eye of doubt on the persons behind the 'Right to Work' measure placed on the Ohio ballot. These are the same persons who down through the years have vigorously fought well-organized attempts to have fair employment measures passed in this state."

Joining Black leaders in mobilizing voters against the right-to-work proposal were many of the state's most influential voices. The Ohio Council of Churches, the United Church of Christ's Council on Christian Social Action, and the Jewish Synagogue Council of America all urged the defeat of Proposal 2. So too did the six Catholic Bishops in the state, while Cleveland Rabbi Abba Silver prepared a special pamphlet to distribute to his congregation. Farris Owens, Vice-President of the Ohio Farm Bureau, and Joseph W. Fichter of the Ohio Farmers' Union worked hard to convince the state's agrarians to vote "no." Fraternal societies like the Eagles, who had stood with labor during the unsuccessful 1955 initiative campaign to reform unemployment compensation, once again demonstrated their support. In Cincinnati, a political newcomer named John J. Gilligan, serving as Chairman of the Citizen's Committee for Economic Stability, placed an ad in the local papers telling "Mrs. Hamilton County Homemaker . . . Don't let 'Right-to-Work' shrink your shopping bag!" Developing an argument also made by other opponents to right-to-work, Gilligan noted that "Official government figures show that in 1956 the typical Ohio family had an income of $2,154 for each member while the typical southern 'Right-to-Work' family had only $1,361 to spend on each member . . . You can protect your family's income by telling women you know what 'Right to Work' really is."

In revised form, Gilligan's essay became one of ten different pamphlets—four million pieces of literature in all—sent to targeted groups around the state. Walter Davis, relying on his knowledge of the radio and television industry, saturated media outlets with United Organized Labor of Ohio's message. He particularly encouraged local TV stations to host debates on the issue. In a pioneering move, United Organized Labor of Ohio purchased a newly developed machine that automatically dialed phone numbers at a rate of 3,000 a day, and played recorded statements against right-to-work by President Harry Truman, former First Lady Eleanor Roosevelt, and such celebrities as comedian Eddie Cantor. This technology, of course, did not replace the lively, old fashion rallies that anti-right-to-work forces held across the state as the election drew near. In mid-September, for instance, twenty-two chartered buses and fifty motor caravans converged for a rally at Veteran's Memorial Auditorium in Columbus. At such gatherings, Elmer Cope marshaled all the theatrics he had learned to denounce supporters of right-to-work as the people "who traditionally have opposed . . . all the social progress of the last 30 years." "The campaign they have waged to get their fraudulent proposal on the ballot . . .," he would quip, "has been clever most of the time, vicious much of the time and unprincipled all of the time." Lines such as these set the crowd cheering.

A major reason why organized labor's campaign against right-to-work was so effective was because United Organized Labor of Ohio employed pollsters — apparently for the first time in such a campaign — to "evaluate the persuasiveness of various arguments presented to Ohio residents uncommitted on the 'Right-to-Work' issue." From the data the pollsters collected, United Organized Labor of Ohio learned, for example, that neither sex nor age was significant factors in determining who supported or opposed the right-to-work amendment. On the other hand, Catholics more often tended to be against, while Protestants were generally for. Hourly and salary workers tended to oppose it; business and professional people were more likely to favor the amendment. Likewise, rural areas were likely to vote "yes," while urban areas would vote "no." Based on this information United Organized Labor of Ohio and other opponents of the amendment were able to target potential voters according their special concerns while the Committee for Proposal 2 was essentially confined to having one strategy for the entire state.

In the waning weeks of the campaign, the Chamber of Commerce and other backers of the right-to-work amendment sought desperately to regain momentum. Apparently using campaign contributions as leverage, on October 14 they were able to get U.S. Senator John Bricker, who had once been Governor of the state and also a vice-presidential candidate, to declare over radio that he would "vote for the Right-to-Work Amendment." Bricker's endorsement came as little surprise because his record was well established as an anti-union defender of the Taft-Hartley Act. Rather, the surprise came when Governor C. William O'Neill went on television on October 21 and publicly tied his re-election campaign to the right-to-work amendment. Both the leadership of the Ohio labor movement, thanks to its pollsters, and of the state's Republican Party knew that opposition as well as support for right-to-work crossed party lines. Now, however, O'Neill and Bricker had made it a Republican issue in the upcoming election. "Sheer stupidity," responded Vice-president Richard Nixon when he learned of O'Neill's endorsement. Ray Bliss, Ohio's GOP Chairman, concluded that whatever hope the Republicans had of winning the gubernatorial and legislative election was now lost.

And so it was. When the polls closed on November 4 and the ballots were counted, both the right-to-work forces and the Republican Party learned that they had been dealt a terrible defeat. Through a well-orchestrated campaign that included unionists and their wives phoning and carpooling hundreds of thousands of targeted voters on election day, Ohioans rejected the right-to-work amendment by a vote of two-to-one. It went down to defeat in every urban, industrial county in the state, although just barely in Franklin County. "I estimate,"

Ohio GOP Chairman Bliss concluded, "that a minimum of 200,000 additional labor Democratic votes went to the polls solely because this issue was on the ballot." And in the process right-to-work pulled down with it almost all of the major Republican candidates in the state. The total gubernatorial vote set a new "off year" record, with Michael DiSalle ousting incumbent O'Neill, and perennial candidate Stephen Young finally replacing the very popular Bricker in the U.S. Senate. The Democrats also captured the Lieutenant Governorship, and the posts of Secretary of State and Treasurer. Likewise, for the first time in over a decade, Democrats sympathetic to labor controlled both houses of General Assembly.

The newly merged labor movement clearly basked in a triumphant beginning. USWA leader Harry Mayfield saw the victory against right-to-work as cementing "the relationship between the AFL and CIO in Ohio." I.W. Abel thought the victory "gave assurance to labor in great states such as Pennsylvania, Illinois, New Jersey and other states of industrial importance that the labor movement meets its opponents and defeats them." Robert Bollard, who became Ohio AFL-CIO Secretary-Treasurer in the early 1960s, thought "that the experience that many of us had in that '58 campaign of Right-to-Work is what really paved the way for us to carry on many more successful campaigns in '64 and in '66 and hopefully still to be carried out." More immediately, a bard on the Ohio AFL-CIO staff — most likely Jane Adams — sent Elmer Cope a Christmas jingle:

We've just caught a long and
dangerous pass
If we don't run with it, somebody
should kick our ass.

Chapter Two

The Ups and Downs of Politics, 1959-1961

I

"These are indeed happy days," proclaimed Ohio AFL-CIO Secretary-Treasurer Elmer Cope at the Federation's January 19, 1959, Legislative Conference. Attended by over 500 unionists from around the state, the conference marked the commencement of labor's efforts to lobby the 103rd Ohio General Assembly. Cope's gleeful remarks to the gathering stemmed from the astounding victory in the November 1958 election in which labor defeated a right-to-work amendment to the Ohio Constitution and helped elect liberal Democratic Governor Michael DiSalle, and, for the first time in over a decade, a pro-labor, Democratic-controlled House and Senate. Even many of the victorious Republicans, including the state's Attorney General William Saxbe, had received Ohio AFL-CIO endorsements. With the prospects of passage of a long list of delayed social and economic reforms, Cope forecasted a new era in Ohio politics marked by concern for the people rather than for business.

Since at least the 1920s, most Ohio politicians and

voters had linked the fate of the state to whatever policies Buckeye businesses felt were best for them — a "what's good for business is good for Ohio" mentality. Even during the disastrously depressed 1930s, both Democratic Governor Martin L. Davey (1935-39) and Republican John Bricker (1939-1945) actively opposed Franklin Delano Roosevelt's New Deal reforms and resisted Ohio's participation in some of the human safety-net programs. The most re-elected Governor in Ohio's history, Democrat Frank Lausche (five times from 1945 to 1957) was as committed to a policy of minimal government, low taxation, and aid to business as was his Republican successor, C. William O'Neill (1957-1959).

In such a political climate, Ohio's businesses boomed in the post-World War II years, making the state second in the nation in industrial output. Yet, such minimal government, low taxation, pro-business policies also stifled Ohio's ability to meet the needs of ordinary citizens. In the late 1950s, the average unemployment contribution rate in Ohio for employers was seventy cents per $100 of payroll while nationally the average stood at $1.31. Naturally, the benefits the system provided suffered accordingly. Likewise, Ohio ranked twenty-fifth in expenditure for primary and secondary education, thirty-fifth in spending on higher education, thirtieth in highway development, twenty-fourth in funding welfare programs, and twenty-eighth for the quality of its hospital and healthcare system. "It had been a long drought in the field of social, economic and labor legislation . . ." Elmer Cope observed. "Now, at long last, there was reason to hope that the harm would be undone. The sky indeed looked bright."

In Columbus on September 23, 1958, labor finalized its political goals for the 103rd General Assembly at an Ohio Committee on Political Education (COPE) meeting. Published in a pamphlet entitled *Common Cause*, the political program contained much that the state's labor movement had championed for years (and would seek for years to come). Several of the planks addressed issues of primary concern to the union movement. These included passage of a "Little" Wagner Act and a "Little" Norris-LaGuardia Law to give Ohio workers engaged in intra-state commerce the same protection to unionize and bargain collectively, free from injunctions, as enjoyed by workers in larger inter-state businesses. The Ohio AFL-CIO also sought the repeal of the Ferguson Act, which limited the union activities of public employees. Most of the provisions of *Common Cause*, however, concerned reforms that would improve life for Ohioans regardless of union status. Ohio labor sought improvements in unemployment and workmen's compensation benefits. It also advocated election law reform to make it easier for citizens to both register and vote, improvements in the state's welfare system, and a restructuring of taxation to improve funding for education. Particular planks of *Common Cause* also reflected the Ohio AFL-CIO's commitment to building a coalition dedicated to advancing social justice. In 1959, the Ohio AFL-CIO once again worked with various African-American groups to establish an Ohio Fair Employment Practices Commission. With its agricultural allies, labor lobbied for legislation that would encourage the family-type farm operation. In tandem with various fraternal groups, the Ohio labor movement fought to outlaw age discrimination in the workplace, to improve aid to the elderly, and to initiate urban housing reform. To a certain extent, then, *Common Cause* anticipated Lyndon Johnson's Great Society by a half decade, but most of the agenda consisted of belated components of Franklin D. Roosevelt's New Deal and Harry Truman's Fair Deal, programs already enacted in other heavily industrialized states.

II

Although the Ohio AFL-CIO prepared to fight aggressively for each plank in *Common Cause,* the most pressing need as the 103rd General Assembly convened in early January 1959 was to amend the state's unemployment compensation law to allow payment of Supplemental Unemployment Benefits (SUBs). This issue revealed clearly why organized labor had to be politically active — a benefit gained through free collective bargaining was being undermined by government edict. The O'Neill administration's decision to forbid the payment of Supplemental Unemployment Benefits in addition to unemployment compensation voided provisions in mutually agreed upon union contracts. The decision also coincided with the 1958 recession, the worst economic downturn to hit Ohio since the Great Depression. As a result, businesses laid off thousands of industrial workers who discovered that their unemployment checks proved inadequate to meet their basic expenses. The struggle by Ohio labor to change the state's policy on SUBs illustrates the complexity of political action by the Ohio AFL-CIO, as the organization had to contest the decision on three fronts: in the General Assembly, in the courts, and at the polls.

In the mid-1950s a number of industrial unions — notably Steelworkers, Autoworkers, Rubber Workers, and Electrical Workers — frustrated at the failure of states to improve unemployment compensation packages, became convinced that the nation's unemployment system would never adequately meet the essential needs of their members. Consequently, they negotiated with their respective industries the creation of supplemental funds to be distributed to the laid-off employees to make up some of the difference between unemployment compensation payments and their former take-home pay. By 1956 SUB programs had been contested in thirteen states outside Ohio, and in each they were found to be acceptable. Nonetheless, in June 1956 the Administrator of the Ohio Bureau of Unemployment Compensation, James R. Tichenor, apparently responding to pressure directly from Governor C. William O'Neill, ruled that an unemployed worker could not receive Supplemental Unemployment Benefits and state unemployment compensation at the same time. Instead, Tichenor decided that the state would deduct any Supplemental Unemployment Benefits from governmental compensation payments.

During 1957, the Ohio CIO, in particular, lobbied the Republican-controlled 102nd General Assembly to amend the law to allow the payment of SUBs in addition to state benefits. The Ohio Advisory Council on Unemployment Compensation (a statutory body appointed by the Governor to recommend changes in the unemployment act) agreed with labor and recommended that the state approve the payment of Supplemental Unemployment Benefits in addition to state compensation. Likewise, representatives from the Ford Motor Company, General Motors Corporation, U.S. Steel, and Youngstown Sheet & Tube testified on behalf of labor. Still, the legislature failed to take action.

Joining Tichenor and the Governor in opposing SUB payments before the General Assembly and later in the courts were the Ohio Chamber of Commerce and the Ohio Information Committee (OIC), an organization representing some 1,000 to 1,500 employers. The Ohio Information Committee had originally organized in 1955 to fight the labor movement's ballot initiative to reform the unemployment system through a constitutional amendment. The Committee's name was meaningless, but its initials —- OIC — were intentionally the CIO in reverse since reversing the progress of the CIO was the organization's aim. The Ohio Information Committee's Executive Secretary, Fred J. Milligan, liked to describe OIC as an antidote to the labor movement. And he defined antidote "as anything that tends to counteract an evil."

Unable to make headway in the state Legislature, on October 3, 1957, the United Steelworkers of America filed a suit in Mahoning County against four major steel companies, Administrator Tichenor, and three key administrative employees of the Youngstown office of the Bureau of Unemployment Compensation. The naming of the four steel companies was a formality, for in actuality they supported labor's stance and joined the unions in arguing for SUB approval. Working closely on this case with USWA attorneys was the legal counsel for the Ohio AFL-CIO, Jacob Clayman, who went on to become national Director of the AFL-CIO Industrial Union Department, and Howard Metzenbaum, who represented Ohio in the United States Senate for two decades beginning in 1974. Their efforts on this case paid off when, on March 5, 1958, Judge Erskine Maiden ruled that the Bureau of Unemployment Compensation did "not have the legal right to reduce the amount of state benefits by the amount of SUB." According to Judge Maiden, Ohio's unemployment compensation law did not forbid "but permits the operation of the Supplemental Unemployment Benefit Plan."

Along with making a declaratory judgment on the law, Judge Maiden also issued a permanent injunction against the continuation of Tichenor's 1956 ruling that a worker could not receive Supplemental Unemployment Benefits in addition to state compensation. Normally, the injunction would have allowed the affected unemployed workers to begin collecting SUB, but in one of several mean-spirited acts during this political battle, Governor O'Neill ordered the Attorney General not only to appeal Judge Maiden's ruling but also to take legal action against the injunction. This meant that Supplemental Unemployment Benefits still would not be dispersed. The Governor could have ordered an appeal of the decision without acting against the injunction and thus permit tens of thousands of unemployed to receive SUB while the legal fight continued. The money would not only have helped them, but would have pumped additional consumer dollars into a sick economy.

Labor won another favorable ruling when on April 16, 1958, the Seventh District Court of Appeals in Youngstown upheld Judge Maiden's March 5 ruling. However, Governor O'Neill still refused to concede and ordered the appellate decision appealed to the Ohio Supreme Court, thus continuing to block SUB payments to eligible unemployed workers. At the May 1958 merger convention of the Ohio AFL-CIO, delegates expressed great frustration at the Governor's actions. Nonetheless, almost all of the delegates believed that with two court decisions supporting Supplemental Unemployment

Benefits, the Ohio Supreme Court would satisfactorily settle the issue, in all probability before the November elections. However, Milligan and the Ohio Information Committee, who worked with the Governor on the appeals, dragged out the fight as long as possible. "It is not our intention," Milligan told the *Cleveland Plain Dealer*, "to waive any time that is provided for in preparation of briefs." Thus, because of the delay, Supplemental Unemployment Benefits joined right-to-work as an issue influencing the outcome of November 1958 election. Indeed, the *Akron Beacon-Journal* opined that in the steel centers of northeastern Ohio, the prohibition of SUB payments, not the right-to-work issue, was "the most important issue against O'Neill."

Organized labor learned another cruel lesson about political life when, on December 3, 1958, the Ohio Supreme Court, by a five-to-two vote, overturned the two lower court decisions and ruled that state law prohibited Supplemental Unemployment Benefits. Ohio AFL-CIO Executive Vice-President Phil Hannah and others condemned the justices as too conservative and hinted that labor would need to work in the next election to assure a more favorable bench. Yet, whatever long-term advantages might come from liberalizing the state's judiciary, the Supreme Court's decision dictated that the Ohio AFL-CIO needed to legalize SUBs during the 1959 legislative session. Had labor not won such an outstanding victory in the November 1958 elections, it is doubtful whether a legislative solution would have been possible.

By March 19, 1959, the Democratic-controlled 103rd General Assembly had passed and newly-elected Governor DiSalle had signed legislation allowing for the simultaneous payment of Supplemental Unemployment

Benefits and state unemployment compensation. In yet another mean-spirited move, however, conservative Republican legislators prevented the law from being designated an emergency measure and thus going into effect immediately. As a consequence, unemployed workers would have to wait another ninety days before getting their due. The public cried out against this bit of nastiness, with Republican State Senator Ross Pepple condemning his colleagues for doing "a cruel thing." Consequently, in early May 1959 a handful of Republicans joined the Democratic majority to pass an emergency bill that at least allowed the payment of the SUB funds held in escrow since the entire controversy began.

The fight to legalize Supplemental Unemployment Benefits was important in its own right, but the struggle also illustrates five features that the Ohio AFL-CIO would confront in future battles. First, this account dramatically shows how politics threatened to undermine a gain originally made through free collective bargaining. Second, it demonstrates how time-consuming the process of changing governmental policy can be, with four years elapsing between Bureau of Unemployment Compensation Administrator Tichenor's decision against Supplemental Unemployment Benefits and the final legislative remedy. Third, the struggle over SUB illustrates how the Ohio AFL-CIO would constantly need to be involved in the administrative, legislative, and judicial aspects of government and that to be effective in these realms it must be a powerful political force. Without the Democratic Party's dramatic victory in the November 1958 elections, it is doubtful if labor would have been able to resolve successfully the SUB crisis. Fourth, in the face of the positive verdicts from two lower courts, the U.S. Internal Revenue Service, and the judicial systems in thirty-seven other states, the Supreme Court's negative decision dramatizes the Ohio AFL-CIO's need to view the judiciary as a highly political body ripe for political change. And finally, the fight over Supplemental Unemployment Benefits, like the concomitant right-to-work fight, reveals the existence in Ohio of an influential group of politicians and businessmen adamantly opposed to organized labor and willing to inflict needless suffering on ordinary people in order to advance narrow self-interests.

III

The Ohio AFL-CIO's success in getting the General Assembly to allow the payment of SUBs was the first of many substantial victories achieved during the 103rd General Assembly. While the Legislature was in session from January to July 1959, the officers and staff of the state body worked feverishly drafting legislation, testifying before committees, conferring with allies, and speaking around the state to mobilize support for *Common Cause*. In addition, Cope and Hannah conducted weekly conferences during which they briefed delegations from local unions and central bodies around the state on pending legislation and then led them in mass into the Statehouse to lobby their local senators and representatives. Elmer Cope also sent out a weekly legislative report to all affiliated units in which he advised them of the status of legislation and badgered them into writing letters to their lawmakers.

The Ohio AFL-CIO's full-court press for *Common Cause* produced spectacular results. The General Assembly improved the Workmen's Compensation Law to increase benefits, allow employees of self-insurers the free choice of doctors, and make it easier for a worker to prove injury on the job. The Legislature also raised the maximum benefits allowed in the state's unemployment compensation program. Likewise, after fourteen years of effort, labor and civil rights advocates secured passage of the Fair Employment Practices Act which prohibited discrimination in employment because of race, color, religion, national origin, or ancestry. The Ohio AFL-CIO also persuaded the General Assembly to improve the state's Aid to the Aged program, to allow voters to re-register by mail, and to permit unions and other groups to set up co-operative medical and dental care plans that would help more people to obtain affordable care.

The Ohio AFL-CIO, however, failed to persuade the 103rd General Assembly to enact all of *Common Cause*. An analysis of the defeated proposals reveals that even in the most favorable political climate certain categories of legislation were going to have a great deal of difficulty ever being enacted. First and foremost, the Ohio AFL-CIO faced an uphill battle in advancing legislation that would place organized labor on a more level playing field with management. This was particularly so of legislation that impacted most on the state's thousands of medium-size and smaller businesses affiliated with the Chamber of Commerce and Milligan's Ohio Information Committee. Thus, the 103rd General Assembly failed to pass a "Little" Wagner Act or a "Little" Norris-LaGuardia Act. The state's small and medium-size businesses, along with their political arm, the Ohio Chamber of Commerce, also resisted the enactment of state minimum wage or maximum hour legislation to cover workers not embraced by federal law. The State Legislature, even when under Democratic control, likewise refused to extend to public employees the rights and benefits enjoyed by workers in private industry. And finally, while people elect legislators, lawmakers always seem reluctant to make it easy for the people to participate in their election. The "liberal" 103rd General Assembly defeated proposals to extend poll hours to 8:00 pm in large, industrial counties to facilitate working-class voting, and also rejected a bill to provide for door-to-door and neighborhood registration.

The leadership of the Ohio AFL-CIO expected to have trouble getting all of *Common Cause* through the Legislature since rural representatives far outnumbered those from industrialized and unionized urban centers. More troubling to them was the fickle behavior of Governor Michael DiSalle. Early in the Governor's term, Elmer Cope told national AFL-CIO General Counsel Arthur Goldberg, "Mike wants to do a thorough, liberal job in the first place and secondly that he intends to build a Democratic Party in the state. Our problem with him will be to help him avoid being too timid in his dealing with us." Cope was right on the mark. DiSalle, the former Mayor of Toledo, was a moderate "liberal" and not a "laborite." During his first year in office he seemed to have misunderstood the dynamics behind his election and sought to stand apart from the state's labor movement. Consequently, in March 1959 he complained to the *Cleveland Plain Dealer* that the leaders of Ohio's labor movement were in too much of a hurry to accomplish in one legislative session "everything they have been denied over a period of time."

Like Senator John F. Kennedy, to whom DiSalle was often compared, the Governor wanted to assert his independence from labor. He failed to support several provisions of *Common Cause* including increasing the state's minimum wage, and vetoed other measures such as reducing the weekly work hours of firemen from seventy-two to fifty-six. More directly, in imitation of Kennedy's role in the McClellan Committee's investigation of "Improper Activities in the Labor and Management Field," DiSalle introduced a "Labor Reform Bill" designed to punish racketeering and corruption in unions. The measure was ill-conceived, outlawing actions that were already illegal, imposing harsher penalties on union leaders than bank presidents and corporate executives would receive for similar offenses, and contradicting federal law in several areas. In the end, the Ohio AFL-CIO persuaded enough representatives to vote against the Governor's proposal to defeat it in the House. But fighting the measure both redirected the lobbying energies of the labor movement and fractured the solidarity of the state Democratic Party.

Whatever shortcomings the Governor or Legislature may have displayed in 1959, however, were clearly outweighed in labor's eyes by some very substantial accomplishments. Shortly after the 103rd General Assembly adjourned, Elmer Cope reflected on its accomplishments.

> As the smoke cleared from one of the most hectic Legislative sessions in history, it was generally agreed that the first Democratic Legislature in 10 years compiled a solid record of achievement in the field of social and economic legislation but fell down badly in the area of basic labor-management relations. On balance it can be said that Ohio workers benefited more from the 103rd General Assembly than from any Legislature in recent years. However, this must be tempered somewhat

with the realization that the Legislature failed to win a tag of 'liberal' Legislature, suffered from a lack of progressive leadership from the Governor's office and House and did not live up to the high hopes that most of us experienced the day after Election Day (November 1958).

At the time he wrote these thoughts, Cope and his colleagues believed that they had laid a foundation upon which future Legislatures would build. Little did he realize that the Ohio AFL-CIO would spend the next several years simply trying to preserve what they had won in those brief six months.

IV

All the while the Ohio AFL-CIO worked to enact *Common Cause*, it was also providing many of its less dramatic, but highly important, services to unionists in the state. The new organization recognized the importance of educating unionists to bolster its cause. Continuing a tradition begun by the Ohio CIO Council in 1945, the Ohio AFL-CIO held its first summer school in July 1958 at Ohio University with 274 unionists in attendance. The 1959 summer school was delayed until after the July 25 adjournment of the 103rd General Assembly and attendance dropped to 162 students, largely due to the absence of steelworkers who were at the time pre-occupied with winning an historic strike. In 1960, summer school attendance again shot up to 279.

Another program carried over from the CIO was the intensive multi-day tutorial for local leaders to prepare them to help members attain benefits from the workmen's compensation and unemployment compensation systems. In December 1958 the Ohio AFL-CIO sponsored its first compensation school with 270 delegates coming to Columbus. The second school, held during the first two weeks of March 1959, had a record-breaking 444 delegates from twenty-eight international unions attending, all eager to master the changes made in the workmen's compensation and unemployment compensation systems by the 1959 legislative session and subsequent court cases. Meanwhile, the Community Services staff of the Ohio AFL-CIO spent considerable time preparing a loose-leaf manual describing each of Ohio's ten public assistance programs as they operated under the new laws. The manual proved a useful guide for local unions trying to cope with welfare problems and also as a text for union counselor training classes. And finally, on April 4, 1959, at the end of a three day labor editor's conference in Columbus sponsored jointly by the Ohio AFL-CIO and the Labor Education and Research Service of The Ohio State University, the delegates established the Ohio Labor Press Association to work for an expanded and more effective labor press in the state.

Increasingly during the Summer, Fall, and into the Winter of 1959, however, the officers and staff of the Ohio AFL-CIO centered their activities on assisting the Steelworkers in their epic 110-day strike. Typically during the 1950s, new contracts had been negotiated in the major industries with little fanfare and few strikes. In 1959, however, the basic steel industry adamantly insisted on a change in work rules and past practices so it could have a free hand in introducing automation into the mills. Unable to reach an agreement on either this point or on wages and benefits, on July 15 a half-million steelworkers — 61,000 of whom lived in Ohio — walked off the job. At first political and community leaders believed that this shutdown would be just another brief strike resolved by a pay raise and a price hike. But their concern began to mount by late August as steel executives remained unyielding and the economy began to suffer from both a reduction in the nation's steel supply and a decline in the steelworkers' purchasing power. The Ohio AFL-CIO joined the rest of the labor movement in financially assisting the strikers and in helping them utilize various community service agencies to meet their most pressing needs. The state body decreed Labor Day, September 7, 1959, as "Support the Steelworkers Day" and sponsored numerous activities to raise funds and rally public opinion. Still the strike dragged on and had a tremendous impact on subsidiary industries in Ohio. Unlike the slugging matches that characterized the famous steel strikes of the 1930s, the 1959 strike was a grim endurance contest in which the powerful steel companies had the greatest reserves. By November 1959 union soup kitchens in Niles, Lorain, Youngstown, and elsewhere fed thousands of strikers and their families and the health of the national economy was threatened. Finally, with no settlement in sight, President Dwight D. Eisenhower received court approval for a ninety-day injunction under provision of the Taft-Hartley Act that sent the strikers back to work on November 7. During the following cooling-off period, USWA leaders made it clear that the union was very willing to re-establish the strike when the ninety days lapsed, and government officials let it be known that they were willing to impose a settlement if none was voluntarily forthcoming. Under such pressure, the steel companies finally capitulated and signed a new agreement giving the workers advances in wages and benefits and leaving work-rules alone.

V

Just as the preeminent concerns of the Ohio AFL-CIO in 1959 were the 103rd General Assembly and the six-month steel strike, election politics dominated 1960. At stake was the presidency of the United States, the make-up of Ohio's delegation to Congress, three seats on the Ohio Supreme Court, and continued Democratic control of the General Assembly. The leadership of the Ohio AFL-CIO was well aware that the Republican Party had been extremely active in rebuilding its base after its defeat in November 1958. Consequently, the state body's Committee on Political Education (COPE) decided to start its political activities as early in the year as possible. Throughout the winter's worst weather, Michael Lyden, Phil Hannah, and Elmer Cope held regional meetings to coordinate labor's political activities on a congressional district basis. Through long experience in the labor movement, all three men were political realists. "There is nothing easy or glamorous about the day-to-day work that keeps Labor safe and permits her to build for the future," Phil Hannah instructed delegates to the regional gatherings. "But no one doubts its necessity or its importance." Likewise, Mike Lyden warned the audiences, "What we were fortunate enough to obtain with the help of many friends in the last Legislature, will be the first target in the next session for the arrows of our opponents. Therefore, we must keep our friends in office and give them some more company."

Political mobilization was also the dominant theme at the Second Constitutional Convention of the Ohio AFL-CIO, held again in Cleveland in June 1960. As planned since the merger, Michael Lyden retired after a half-century of service to the labor movement. The convention abolished the office of Executive Vice-President, elevated Phil Hannah to the presidency, and retained Elmer Cope as Secretary-Treasurer. Along with reaffirming and enriching the political program, *Common Cause,* the delegates listened to speaker after speaker, including Emil Mazey of the Autoworkers and I.W. Abel of the Steelworkers, challenge them to repeat in November 1960 the victory enjoyed two years earlier.

Organized labor campaigned hard during the Summer and Fall of 1960. Following strategies developed for the 1958 campaign, the Ohio AFL-CIO mounted a massive registration drive, targeting Columbus, Springfield, Cincinnati, Dayton, Toledo, Canton, Akron, and Cleveland. Once again the Women's Activities Department checked registrations, distributed literature, made phone calls, and staffed precincts on election day. At its September meeting, Ohio COPE formally endorsed the national Kennedy-Johnson ticket. At the state level, COPE truly honored its slogan that "political labels are secondary. Voting records are primary." It endorsed two Republicans and one Democrat for seats on the Ohio Supreme Court. In the only other statewide race, that for Auditor, COPE supported both Democrat James Ferguson and his Republican opponent James Rhodes. As election day drew near, the Federation initiated the final stages of the 'get-out-the-vote' campaign with telephone calls, sample ballots, and car pools.

After the polls closed on November 4, however, it quickly became apparent that organized labor in Ohio had suffered a significant setback. Not only had Ohio failed to support Kennedy for the presidency, but the GOP recaptured both houses of the General Assembly and picked up two additional Congressional seats. A number of factors accounted for labor's poor showing. Robert Bollard, who in a few years would succeed Elmer Cope as Ohio AFL-CIO's Secretary-Treasurer, contended that in 1960 there was a relaxation of effort at the local level after the triumph in the 1958 right-to-work election. Ray Ross and other participants commented on the difficulty of mobilizing union voters since there was no gubernatorial race or high-powered issue to bring them out. While all these issues were probably at work, a major factor in shaping the election's outcome, especially in regards to the state's legislative races, was the gross misapportionment of the state's legislative districts. The Ohio Constitution provided that each county in the state would have at least one representative in the Legislature. Consequently, while the eleven urban districts in the state in 1960, containing over five million inhabitants, elected only sixty-two state representatives, rural districts with only three million residents filled seventy-seven seats in the House. No matter how many union voters went to the polls, under such an apportionment scheme labor could seldom gain control of the General Assembly. In November 1958, the Ohio AFL-CIO had been victorious because right-to-work was a statewide issue on which the total state vote counted, and because a number of factors contributed to keeping voter turnout in rural areas low. In November 1960, however, the presidential election helped stimulate high voter participation in the less populated but over represented areas.

Clearly, the election foretold of hard times ahead for labor. Fortunately, however, friendly Democrats still controlled the administrative branch of government, since three years earlier the voters had amended the Ohio Constitution to provide for a four year rather than two year gubernatorial term. Michael DiSalle would spend the second half of his governorship wielding a veto to preserve the gains labor had won during his first two years in office. Likewise, even though the majority of justices on the state Supreme Court were Republicans, the Ohio AFL-CIO's commitment to supporting its friends regardless of party label meant that it could count on some support on cases that made it to Ohio's highest tribunal.

VI

Labor's mindset as the 104th General Assembly convened contrasted sharply with the hopefulness and optimism with which it had greeted the convening of the 103rd General Assembly. "The mood," Elmer Cope related, "was one of apprehension." Believing that the best defense was a strong offense, the Ohio AFL-CIO aggressively challenged the incoming Legislature to enact labor's political program. Cope, as the organization's chief legislative agent, constantly applied pressure on the lawmakers. During 1961, he mailed out twelve *Legislative Reports* to locals detailing measures before the General Assembly and asking for grass-roots lobbying. The Ohio AFL-CIO also ran a weekly series of radio shows on thirty stations around the state to inform the public about its stance on measures before the Legislature, particularly those dealing with unemployment compensation. During March and April — the heart of the legislative session — the Ohio AFL-CIO conducted seven weekly conferences designed to both present a united lobby before the Legislature and to serve as a conduit to getting labor's story across back at home. Each conference lasted three days, with the delegates contacting their local state representatives and senators.

Throughout the legislative session of 1961, the Ohio AFL-CIO ended up battling just as vigorously to protect its earlier gains, as it did to achieve them in the first place. Republican leaders ignored the Democrat/ Ohio AFL-CIO legislative program, failing to hold hearings on many proposals and twisting the contents of other pro-worker bills so out of shape that in the end labor ended up opposing them. The most noted casualties of these tactics were proposals to improve and reform the state's unemployment compensation program.

Beginning in 1957, unemployment in Ohio began climbing, reaching 8.6 percent by January 1961. At labor's urging, immediately following the November 1960 election, Governor DiSalle called the 103rd General Assembly back into special session in hope that the Democratic-dominated body would extend unemployment benefits from twenty-six to thirty-nine weeks. But two Democrats joined solid Republican opposition to prevent any measure being passed by the short session. When the 104th General Assembly convened during the first week in January 1961, the number of Ohioans receiving unemployment compensation had climbed for the thirteenth straight week, with the number setting a new record high shortly afterwards. Initially the Republican majority opposed any bill to extend coverage for additional weeks. But when they realized that the Kennedy Administration was about to enact national legislation granting an extension, the state's Republicans backtracked, approved a thirteen week extension, yet added provisions that actually established a "needs test" and reduced the number of workers eligible for coverage. The Ohio AFL-CIO vociferously denounced these maneuvers to downscale the state's unemployment compensation system and staged a massive rally at the

Statehouse on March 5 supporting DiSalle's veto of the act.

The Republican majority again sought to pare the unemployment compensation program when the General Assembly took up the challenge of restoring the shrinking fund to a sound condition. Back in 1953, with post-World War II prosperity and full employment, the fund had been in excellent condition. But employers — pointing to the millions of dollars the fund had in reserve — convinced the Republican-controlled Legislature to cut employers' contribution rates, even though Ohio employer contributions to the fund had for years already been below the national average. The 1953 employer rate reductions were so substantial that in no year between 1953 and 1960 had payments to the fund covered disbursements. With reduced revenue coming in and with larger amounts being paid out as unemployment rose during the recession that gripped Ohio from 1958 to 1961, the state's fund approached insolvency. Yet, efforts to increase the employer contribution rates to put the fund on a more secure footing met solid Republican opposition. And when the GOP leadership finally agreed to take a half-step toward resolving the crisis, they insisted that coverage under the law be greatly restricted. Once again, the Ohio AFL-CIO found itself relying on a gubernatorial veto to preserve the system.

Republicans repeated the scenario on unemployment compensation when other labor issues came before the 104th General Assembly. Claiming a desire to close "loopholes" which promoted "frivolous and fraudulent claims," the Republican-controlled General Assembly attempted to rewrite the Workmen's Compensation Law to the point that the *Dayton Daily News* exclaimed that "the remedy is worse than the malady" The Legislature also assaulted the limits on the number of consecutive hours women could work, dragged its feet on extending aid to dependent children, and denied unemployment compensation to Great Lakes seamen. Not surprisingly, Elmer Cope concluded that "the 104th General Assembly was an exercise in frustration and disappointment for the Ohio workers." Since its ecstatic victory in November 1958, the Ohio AFL-CIO had clearly experienced the ups and downs of politics.

The new officers of the Ohio AFL-CIO join hands at the 1958 merger convention. From left are Secretary-Treasurer Elmer Cope, President Michael Lyden, and Executive Vice President Phil Hannah. (Ohio AFL-CIO)

Delegates listen to the proceedings at the 1958 merger convention in Cleveland's Public Hall. (Ohio AFL-CIO Collection at the Ohio Historical Society)

AFL-CIO Secretary-Treasurer William Schnitzler (second from right) presents the Ohio AFL-CIO's new charter to (from left) Michael Lyden, Elmer Cope, Phil Hannah, and Ray Ross, the President of the Ohio CIO Council. (Ohio AFL-CIO Collection at the Ohio Historical Society)

Ray Ross, Phil Hannah, Ohio CIO Council Secretary-Treasurer John Rooney, and Michael Lyden confer during the merger convention (Ohio AFL-CIO Collection at the Ohio Historical Society)

The members of the Ohio AFL-CIO's first Executive Board. Seated (left to right) are Paul Schremp, John S. Johns, Paul Rusen, Marty Hughes, Phil Hannah, Michael Lyden, Elmer Cope, Pat O'Malley, Ray Ross, Joe Mullahy. Standing (left to right) are Art Kistemaker, Joe Gembus, Edgar Baker, Leo Dugan, Charles Romine, Herschel White, Henry Seibert, Matthew DeMore, Sebastian Lupica, and William Goldberg. (Ohio AFL-CIO)

Michael Lyden, Elmer Cope, and Phil Hannah campaign against the "right to work" measure. (Elmer Cope Collection at the Ohio Historical Society)

Elmer Cope meeting with Governor Michael DiSalle (left) and United Steelworkers General Counsel Arthur Goldberg (center) during the 1959 Steelworkers strike. (Elmer Cope Collection at the Ohio Historical Society)

Elmer Cope debating the Ohio Chamber of Commerce's Herschel Atkinson before a state-wide television audience. (Elmer Cope Collection at the Ohio Historical Society)

Chapter Three

The Turmoil of Democracy: 1961-1966

I

Frustration and disappointment clearly characterized the mood of the Ohio AFL-CIO Executive Board in the early months of 1961. Having received accolades from columnists for its dramatic electoral success in 1958, board members now read barbed editorials about the organization's fleeting strength and its inability in 1960 either to retain hold of the General Assembly or to carry Ohio for John F. Kennedy — one of the few times in the twentieth century that the Buckeye State failed to cast its vote with the winning presidential candidate.

Seeking a way to reverse labor's misfortunes at an April 14, 1961, meeting, the Executive Board unanimously approved a proposal by Jim Griffin of the Steelworkers to create a new position, that of Director of Political Education. To fill the post, the Executive Board turned to one of its own members, Morris Riger, who was also the United Textile Workers of America's Regional Director for Ohio and Michigan. Active in progressive causes in the Cleveland area, Riger possessed a reputation as a creative thinker and a hard worker. Over the Summer of 1961 he researched and consulted extensively with numerous individuals in order to devise a strategy for more effective voter mobilization in Ohio. On September 28 Riger presented his inch-thick report entitled *Blueprint for Victory* to the Ohio AFL-CIO Executive Committee (a steering committee of the Executive Board) and then on the following day to the entire Executive Board.

Blueprint for Victory proposed the creation of a separate political education office within the state body headed by a director and staffed by eight full-time regional directors. This staff would oversee extensive voter registration activities with the goal of allowing the state office both to contact and to monitor the voting behavior of every Ohio trade unionist. The political education staff would also work directly with central bodies, retiree groups, and the Women's Activities Division to educate union members on issues before the Ohio General Assembly as well as the U.S. Congress.

Riger had devised an impressive plan that received the Executive Board's approval with only a few reservations. Those were made largely by John S. Johns of the Steelworkers, who worried that in approving *Blueprint for Victory* the Ohio AFL-CIO would create a staff independent of any of the elected officers. At the Executive Board meeting no one expressed concern that the new program called for a three cents increase in the per capita dues affiliates paid to the Ohio AFL-CIO, to be placed in a separate political education fund to maintain the program. Rather, in September 1961 most of the state body's leadership felt they would be presenting to the May 1962 Ohio AFL-CIO convention a very dynamic proposal that would reverse the organization's political fortunes.

By January 1962, however, discontent with *Blueprint for Victory* increased. A diverse set of factors attributed to this rising concern. For one, several Executive Board members who had abstained from voting at the September meeting out of a desire to first consult with their unions had studied the document closely and concluded that the three cents per capita tax increase was both too much for their organizations to afford and too little to do the job actually outlined in *Blueprint*. Rather, they believed that approving the program would begin an upward spiral of per capita increases without ever accomplishing the goals. Secondly, some Board members began to concur in John Johns' view that *Blueprint for Victory* gave the Director of Political Education "too broad authority," including control over an independent staff.

The behavior of Morris Riger reinforced this latter view. Riger saw Elmer Cope as the obstacle to effective political action and worked to undermine the Secretary-Treasurer's authority. He had no trouble finding allies among people and unions either angered with Cope's rather bullish personal behavior, upset by the dominant position of the Steelworkers within the Ohio AFL-CIO, or who simply wanted the state body to assume a more aggressive political posture. A group of autoworkers, led by former CIO President Ray Ross, wanting both a political action program modeled on the UAW and a more prominent role for the Autoworkers in the state organization, actively supported Riger. So too did Ohio AFL-CIO's incumbent President Phil Hannah who, according to the *Columbus Dispatch*, "had been at swords point" with Cope "almost since the start of the AFL-CIO merger." Deciding that the best strategy was to confront Cope head on, Morris Riger announced in early Spring

1962 that he would challenge Cope for the position of Secretary-Treasurer at the upcoming convention. To many people's surprise, Phil Hannah elected to join Riger on a united ticket. *Blueprint for Victory* now became a campaign program for a specific caucus within the organization.

The mood at the 1962 Ohio AFL-CIO convention, which convened in Cleveland on May 22, was one of tension yet civility. Both Phil Hannah and Elmer Cope publicly displayed the utmost courtesy throughout the sessions, and almost all of the speakers showed remarkable restraint. No one really knew which way the political winds would blow when the ballots were counted, but everyone realized that the vote on the *Blueprint for Victory* program would likely forecast the subsequent election of officers. Debate on the program lasted all of Wednesday afternoon, with Hannah making sure that each side had an equal opportunity to speak. By far the most forceful remarks came from John S. Johns, who painstakingly detailed how the three cents increase in per capita tax would not even cover the administrative and equipment costs of the plan. A number of delegates from smaller locals further argued that instead of increasing the per capita tax in order to fund the program, the state body should first get the hundreds of unaffiliated locals to join the Ohio AFL-CIO, thereby both increasing numerical strength and the treasury of the state body. Proponents of *Blueprint for Victory*, on the other hand, charged the program's critics with "being penny-wise and PAC-foolish." At the end of the protracted debate, Joe Hyde, a delegate from UAW Local 785, wisely moved to postpone the vote until the following morning to allow people to "cool off."

The next morning Secretary-Treasurer Elmer Cope began the laborious but important process of conducting a roll-call vote. Over four hours later, he announced the defeat of *Blueprint for Victory* by a vote of 279,526 to 205,681, no doubt with a private sense of pleasure. An analysis of the voting reveals only vague patterns of fleeting import. Autoworkers were the single largest union in favor (although Richard Gosser and the Toledo autoworkers stood opposed). On the other hand most rubber workers, hotel and restaurant workers, retail clerks, and steelworkers voted against the plan (although James P. Griffin of USWA District 26 was a chief sponsor). Most other organizations, whether from the old AFL or the CIO, divided their votes freely. Indeed, the geographic base of the delegates seemed as important as affiliation in determining voting behavior, with the northern part of Ohio (except Toledo) supporting *Blueprint for Victory* and delegates from the central and southern regions more likely to be opposed. This may have something to do with the "spheres of influence" of the various backers and opponents to the plan, but even that is not clear.

What was clear was that Morris Riger's chances to replace Elmer Cope as Secretary-Treasurer were doomed even before the afternoon voting took place. When the propitious moment came, the incumbent Cope defeated the challenger Riger by over a thousand votes.

Less clear was the fate of Phil Hannah. Opponents of the Riger-Hannah ticket had waited until the convention had begun to target a candidate to run against Hannah, and that person was the little known David Kane. A youthful redhead with a personable smile, Kane was born in Pennsylvania in 1922, but moved with his family to Zanesville when he was only two. After high school he worked at Zanesville Pottery Company until he enlisted in the Army during World War II. Serving for three and a half years as a radio officer with the Office of Strategic Services, Kane participated in sabotage activities behind enemy lines and took part in the invasions of both North Africa and southern France. After the war he obtained a job as an apprentice bookbinder at the McCall Corporation in Dayton. Becoming a journeyman bookbinder, in November 1958 he was elected Business Agent of the 1,500 member Bookbinders Local 199 in Dayton and a year later he also assumed the presidency of the Ohio Bookbinders Conference, made up of twelve unions.

Why Cope selected Kane as his running mate for the presidency can only be guessed. For one, Kane personified the smaller unions and the empowerment of the average delegate. For another, he came from the Dayton-Springfield area which in 1958 under Breidenback had opposed merger and now was part of Ray Ross' "sphere of influence." And finally, tired of the tug-of-war between President Hannah and Secretary-Treasurer Cope, several members of the Executive Board were anxious to have an officer willing to play second fiddle.

Still, Hannah retained the respect and popularity of many delegates who otherwise opposed his support for Riger and the *Blueprint*. In the end, he lost by a mere fifty-seven votes (out of a total of 4,700 votes cast). Irven Scheiber of the *Columbus Dispatch* credited Hannah's defeat to "many leaders of former AFL unions" who "still resented the active role Hannah played in merger negotiations." In particular various leaders of the building trades, "never forgot their grudge against Hannah and no doubt welcomed the opportunity . . . to shoot him out of the saddle." Scheiber's analysis might have been right, but the larger reality was that Riger dragged most of his supporters down to defeat with him. In the voting for Executive Board members, for instance, twenty-four candidates on the Cope slate won, while only four on the Hannah-Riger ticket became Vice Presidents.

While there were individual winners and losers at the 1962 convention, the Ohio AFL-CIO emerged as the ultimate victor. Whether *Blueprint for Victory* would have given Ohio labor more political muscle is a question history cannot settle. What is clear is that four years after merger, the Ohio AFL-CIO engaged in the thrusts and jabs of the democratic process and stood the test. The coalitions that squared off in 1962 were not simply the old AFL versus CIO, but new groupings based on new issues. And when the quarreling was done the organization emerged intact. No one stormed out of the convention nor disaffiliated. Rather they all stayed around, if only to fight another day. And in advancing the healing process, much credit needs to be given to Phil Hannah who never lost his dignity and his respect for the delegates. "I want to thank each and everyone of you who supported me," Hannah related in his conceding remarks. "I want to thank those who voted against me, because under the circumstances, probably they made the right decision. Therefore, I leave you with love, respect, devotion."

II

Emerging from the turmoil of internal democracy, the Ohio AFL-CIO immediately focused on the upcoming November 1962 election. On July 25, following Morris Riger's resignation as Director of Political Education, the

Executive Board appointed Edward W. Bodi of the UAW to take his place. The Board also approved a new political education program that borrowed heavily from the defeated *Blueprint for Victory* in emphasizing statewide coordination and planning. It too called for the extensive use of the Women's Activities Division and retiree groups, as well as having a political education coordinator in each congressional district to organize activities of international unions, central bodies, locals, and COPE organizations. And as in previous elections, COPE launched a massive registration and get out the vote drive.

Yet despite an impressive effort in 1962, the Ohio AFL-CIO failed to check the continuing Republican drift in state politics. DiSalle was burdened in his re-election campaign by his qualms about the death penalty, which led to several sensational commutations, and even more by his need to push through a tax increase to keep the state solvent after a decade of underfunding by the parsimonious Lausche and O'Neill administrations. His opponent, James A. Rhodes, quickly made political hay by dubbing him "TAX-HIKE MIKE." The *Troy Daily News* appropriately summed up DiSalle's re-election predicament when it wrote: "This is an essentially conservative state, after all. One observer has remarked, 'It should be noted that the average citizen of Ohio is very strongly in favor of progress. All he is opposed to is paying for that progress.' And Mike DiSalle, thanks to his enemies, is firmly associated in the mind of John and Jane Buckeye with the idea of paying for that progress."

Not only did Michael DiSalle lose by a substantial margin to Rhodes, but the Democrats lost even more seats in both the Ohio House and Senate. Consequently, gains that Ohio workers had realized through the 1959 General

Assembly and preserved against the 1961 Legislature thanks to the vetoes of a Democratic Governor, were largely wiped out by the Republican-controlled 1963 Legislature. Throughout the 105th General Assembly, the Republican majority gave employer legislation priority and ignored labor's program.

Once again, the lawmakers did the employers' bidding in weakening both the unemployment and the workmen's compensation system by cutting benefits and eligibility. The cuts in unemployment insurance alone amounted to over $16 million dollars a year. Unable to stop the Republican juggernaut in the General Assembly, the leaders of the Ohio AFL-CIO pinned their hopes on a massive rally in Columbus that would remind Governor Rhodes of his campaign pledge of "no harsh anti-union legislation" and persuade him to veto the measures. On May 15, 1963, 10,000 unionists, their families, and friends participated in the largest labor demonstration in Ohio history up to that time. Thirty-five years later, Warren Smith, a future Secretary-Treasurer of the state body, still recalled the thrill of watching the solid phalanx encircle the State House, waving signs reading "Don't Lynch the Unemployed" and chanting "Save Ohio's Compensation System." Yet dramatic as the rally was, the lesson learned by Smith and others was that such displays rarely carry the day. Future Ohio AFL-CIO President Frank W. King instructed local unionists several years later: "It's a sad note that the demonstration did not change one word in that unemployment bill. The point to remember about that incident is that in the political arena your activity and backing only counts **before** the election, not after it." And so it was the case, as Governor Rhodes maintained his alliance with the employers and approved all of their proposals that cleared the Legislature.

Organized labor rapidly gained the measure of James A. Rhodes, a man who would be a power in state politics for the next twenty years. Born in Jackson County and reared in Springfield, as a young man Rhodes settled in Columbus where he briefly attended Ohio State University. From early adulthood Rhodes was a hustler and a huckster in business and politics. As Mayor of Columbus in the late 1940s and early 1950s, Rhodes had received the endorsement of the city's labor movement for his willingness to support the Steelworkers in their organizing drive against Timken. Likewise, his criticism of the right-to-work forces in 1958 won him a COPE endorsement when he ran for re-election as State Auditor in 1960.

Viewing himself as a moderate Republican, Rhodes publicized his humble origins while always gratifying the wants of the business class. He firmly believed that Ohio would prosper economically if the government kept the state cheap for business to operate in. A master of collapsing complex issues into one-line slogans, he sought to attract new businesses by proclaiming that "Profit is not a dirty word in Ohio," and that he would allow "no new taxes." Increasing jobs, he contended would alleviate the need to raise rates for the state's unemployment compensation system. Likewise, if education and social services required increased funding, that would come through expanding the state's tax base by encouraging business growth. And if Ohio required a better infrastructure to attract businesses, such improvements should be paid for through long-term bonds payable by the next generation, whom Rhodes simply assumed would be more prosperous.

Organized labor did not so much object to Rhodes'

ends — expanding Ohio's economy — as it deplored his means — placing the cost on lower and middle income citizens and on their children and grandchildren. Indeed, Rhodes' massive state-funded building programs actually won him strong support from many workers in the building trades. Unlike a future generation of Ohio Republicans, moreover, Rhodes desired to modify organized labor's political influence, not to vanquish it. While fighting labor on most issues, he would also seek some cause where an alliance could be made. Still, Rhodes played political hardball, with labor usually on the opposing team. David Kane, a novice at political affairs when elected President of the Ohio AFL-CIO, was unprepared for Rhodes' candor when he lobbied the Governor in 1963 to veto pending unemployment and workmen's compensation laws. "We had a meeting with our 'good friend' Governor Rhodes," Kane later reported. "After twenty five minutes of his 'hogwash', and everything, he finally tells us, 'Look, fellows, you have lost an election, suffer the consequences.' As the meeting broke up, he put his hand on Joe Murphy's (Building Service Employees) shoulder and Tom McDonald's (Structural Iron Workers, both of whom had supported Rhodes) and said, 'These two boys I have allegiance to.' After we walked out, they stood back and had their little conference."

III

While the Ohio AFL-CIO's inability to modify the policies of Governor Rhodes and the 1963 General Assembly grew directly out of the Democrats bad showing in the 1962 elections, the organization also suffered from a crisis in its own leadership. David Kane assumed the presidency inexperienced in political affairs but eager to become engaged. Elmer Cope, however, saw himself as the voice of labor before the Legislature and sent Kane touring Ohio in an effort to get unaffiliated unions to join the state body. Yet illnesses kept Cope from working at full strength. Whereas during previous sessions of the General Assembly, Cope churned out voluminous reports and letters, his records for 1963 are surprisingly sparse. Finally, on August 1, ill-health forced Cope to resign and move back to Pittsburgh, where he worked whenever he could as an educational consultant with the USWA. He died on May 26, 1965.

The Ohio AFL-CIO Executive Board now had to find an acceptable replacement for Cope, one who might help heal wounds still festering after the contentious 1962 convention. Power realities dictated that the post would again go to a Steelworker, since the USWA was the largest union in the state. However, most of that union's state leadership had been very visible in the Elmer Cope-Morris Riger fight. Thus emerged Robert "Bob" Bollard. Born in 1922, Bollard had began work at seventeen in the packing houses of Fort Dodge, Iowa, and immediately became a union activist. From 1946 to 1948 he was Assistant Editor and Educational Director for the Packinghouse Workers' International Union in Chicago. Then, in 1948 he transferred over to the Illinois Industrial Union Council where he served as legislative officer, editor of its newspaper, and educational representative. Eight years later, Bollard left that post to join the United Steelworkers, District 25 in Cincinnati as a staff representative responsible for education and public relations. While an accomplished individual, Bollard was not well known to Ohio unionists beyond those belonging to the Steelworkers.

In an interview years later, Bollard would comment on the irony of how a hernia operation prevented him from attending the divisive 1962 convention. "I turned out to be Mr. Clean," he joked, "in that I was not identified with that big fight. No one ever knew what position I would have taken had I been at the convention. And I hadn't gained bad friends or any bad taste in anybody's mouth." When Bollard met with Executive Board members prior to his appointment, he impressed them with his determination to build greater unity within the state body. "I heard that after I was excused from that interview," he related, "that many of the members of the executive board commented on my reference to team effort; and that is exactly what they were looking for at the time: someone who could pick up the marbles and mold them together into a cohesive team effort."

During his tenure as Secretary-Treasurer, Bollard spent considerable time building programs to service affiliates and union members even when labor's clout with the Statehouse waned. He continued the annual two-week conferences on unemployment insurance and workers' compensation, and added programming on Social Security. Under Bollard's initiative, by May 1964, the state body's assistance on Social Security disability claims had risen to exceed the number of unemployment insurance claims it helped process. In April 1964, Bollard also resuscitated the Ohio Labor Press Association, which had been dormant since 1960. He also resurrected the Ohio AFL-CIO Summer School, which had ceased convening after 1960 because organizers believed that it conflicted with programs held by various internationals. In July 1966, seventy-nine students from seventeen international unions wandered the backroads to Gambier, Ohio, for the first of a long line of summer schools held at bucolic Kenyon College. Bollard took greatest pride, however, in his role in establishing statewide civil rights meetings beginning in the fall of 1963 and in developing the Ohio AFL-CIO Community Services Activities. Inspired by President Lyndon Johnson's "War on Poverty" and working closely with Executive Board member Ray Ross, who chaired the state body's Community Services Committee, Bollard organized the first Community Services Activities Conference in January 1964. By the time of the Ohio AFL-CIO's June 1966 convention, the community services activities had expanded to the point that the organization established the Community Services Department with the prime goal of acquainting union members with the work of social agencies available in their own local communities.

While Bollard took special delight in internal program building, he also pushed labor's political interests. Stymied in advancing specific legislation by Republican control of the governorship and the General Assembly, Bollard's greatest success came through increasing the Ohio AFL-CIO's influence in the state's Democratic Party. After their defeat in the November 1962 election, the Democrats were in disarray. The Ohio AFL-CIO had no desire to take over the party, but labor was the most organized and focused component of a disorganized coalition. Bollard led unionists into the vacuum and increased labor's influence over the party. Consequently, whereas the Ohio delegation to the 1960 Democratic National Convention had contained only two unionists, the 1964 delegation included eight labor leaders as regular delegates and another eight as alternates.

In contrast to the accomplishments of Bollard,

President David Kane floundered. Despite his efforts to increase affiliations with the state body, his results were no better than those of everyone else who has tried, before or since. He was also a novice at lobbying the Legislature at a time when the union movement needed an accomplished hand. "It has been a real experience," Kane would later admit. "It has been two years of college in political science." Increasingly, various members of the Executive Board concluded that they needed someone more in command of political affairs and who represented a larger union with greater influence both within the labor movement and externally. By the Spring of 1964 they had persuaded Frank W. King to challenge Kane for the presidency.

King clearly presented a different profile than Kane. Born in 1912, King grew up in the Toledo area where he became an apprentice bricklayer at the age of sixteen. As a member of the Bricklayers, Masons and Plasters Union for thirty-six years, King was linked to the powerful building trades unions whose reluctant ties to the merged Ohio AFL-CIO still needed tightening. Indeed, the Ohio State Building and Construction Trades Council would not formally affiliate with the Ohio AFL-CIO until after King's election. King was also a twenty-five year member of the American Federation of Teachers, another growing voice in the state's labor movement. Equally important though, King had long experience in state politics and Democratic Party affairs, having won a seat from Toledo in the Ohio House in 1949 and then a seat in the State Senate in 1954. As Senate Majority Leader of the Democratic-controlled 103rd General Assembly, King oversaw the passage of the most favorable labor legislation in decades. Then, as Senate Minority Leader in the two subsequent General Assemblies, he had worked closely with the leadership of the Ohio AFL-CIO to forestall reverses as best as possible.

While King appeared an attractive candidate to replace Kane as President, some delegates to the Ohio AFL-CIO's May 1964 convention questioned whether he was willing to give up his Senate seat to work full-time for the organization as the constitution required. The backers of King, particularly Charles Ballard of the Toledo-area UAW, delicately explained to delegates that King would resign from the Senate, but only after the November elections. If King resigned before the election, then both Republicans and Democrats would put up candidates to replace him with uncertain results. If he waited until after the election to step down, then the Democrats alone would be empowered to appoint a replacement. With delegates satisfied on this point, Frank King won the presidency over David Kane, 3,334 votes to 1,279. Bob Bollard, who stayed neutral in the presidential contest, was unanimously elected Secretary-Treasurer. Hoping to avoid a repeat of the tensions that had existed between Elmer Cope and Phil Hannah, the convention amended the constitution to emphasize the President's role as a lobbyist and the Secretary-Treasurer's responsibility as a staff supervisor. The vaguely worded amendment, however, failed to settle the division of authority, for the issue would reappear again in the not so distant future.

IV

Both Frank King and Bob Bollard left the 1964 convention determined to reverse the setbacks labor had suffered at the polls in the 1960 and 1962. In preparing for the November 1964 election, they employed previously developed strategies to register voters, increase awareness of the candidate's strengths and weaknesses, and mobilize the vote on election day. This time, however, broad social and political developments made union members, in particular, and the voting public, in general, far more receptive to labor's efforts. On the one hand, ultra-conservatives led by Arizona Senator Barry Goldwater captured the national Republican Party. Goldwater disturbed many voters with his libertarian proclamations that government should not dispense welfare, tax incomes on a progressive basis, aid public education, or be involved with the popular Social Security system. Concomitantly, in the area of foreign policy and military affairs, he presented himself as all-too-eager to launch a nuclear attack against any Communist foe, big or small. On the other hand, Lyndon B. Johnson portrayed himself as a responsible moderate, choosing Minnesota's liberal Senator Hubert Humphrey to balance the ticket. His summons to build a "Great Society" in which poverty and racial injustice no longer existed captured the imagination of many Americans in this year of optimism before race riots, campus protests, and the Vietnam War dominated the nation's headlines. As a result, Johnson won re-election by a landslide, receiving sixty-one percent of the vote and carrying every state except Arizona and four in the deep South. Throughout the country, in local and state contests, moderate and liberal Democrats rode to victory on LBJ's "coattails."

In Ohio, organized labor was ecstatic. Led by the one-million vote state margin for Johnson, labor-endorsed candidates won more contests in the November 3 voting than in any balloting since the "right to work" year of 1958. Along with carrying the state for a Democratic presidential candidate for the first time since 1948, the

Ohio AFL-CIO helped re-elect U.S. Senator Stephen M. Young to a second term and sent two additional Democrats to Congress. More important for its own lobbying efforts, the Ohio AFL-CIO aided the Democratic Party in reducing the Republican majority in the Ohio House by thirteen seats and in neutralizing the GOP in the Senate through a sixteen to sixteen tie. With undue modesty, the retiring Editor of *News and Views*, Don Smith, judged the outcome "on the whole a fairly successful election."

The parity between the Republicans and Democrats in the Ohio Senate, however, created a quandary for the Ohio AFL-CIO Executive Board. Frank King had promised to resign his Senate seat following the election to devote his full energies to the Ohio AFL-CIO. Yet with the parties equally balanced at sixteen senators each, and with seventeen votes needed to pass legislation it now seemed unwise for King to abandon his role as Senate Democratic leader and turn his seat over to a novice. At an emergency meeting on November 20, 1964, the Executive Board wisely placed reason over rules and asked King to remain in the Senate for the next session.

During the 106th General Assembly, which convened in January 1965, Frank King adroitly utilized the sixteen to sixteen tie in the Senate to block Republican efforts to push additional anti-labor legislation. But by the same token the Ohio AFL-CIO made no progress in advancing its program, save for a tame fair housing bill and a long-overdue revamping of the welfare system. The significant political drama in the Winter and Spring of 1965, then, occurred not at the Statehouse but in the polling booths during the May primary election, and the issue would be legislative reapportionment.

V

The 1965 battle over reapportionment began in 1903 when Ohio voters passed the Hanna amendment to the state constitution guaranteeing each county at least one representative in the Ohio House, regardless of its population. Representation in the Ohio Senate though was kept on a population basis. Over the years, the Hanna amendment greatly strengthened the political clout of rural, anti-union areas. "The way Congressional and General Assembly district lines are drawn," an Ohio COPE circular noted, "often determine the outcome of an election before the first vote is cast." As a result of the Hanna amendment, by the early 1960s, less than a third of Ohio's population elected a majority of the state's representatives. Each member of the Ohio House from Cleveland's Cuyahoga County, for instance, represented 100,000 people, compared to the House member from rural Vinton County, who represented only 10,270 folks. Such malapportionment clearly undermined labor's ability to alleviate its woes through legislative remedies. A report done for the Ohio AFL-CIO in the early 1960s showed that representatives from low population counties traditionally opposed labor's position by a ration of two to one, while House members from heavily populated, urban counties supported labor's position by a ratio of three to one. Clearly for organized labor to have greater legislative success the method used to apportion House seats would have to change.

Ohio's malapportionment reflected a national problem, with election districts throughout the country gerrymandered as much to weaken the political voice of African-Americans as of white, urban industrial workers. With the rise of the civil rights movement in the 1950s, however, various organizations and individuals initiated challenges to unequal representation through the court system. In Ohio, James Nolan of Cleveland brought an action in the Federal District Court at Cincinnati, complaining that the Hanna amendment diluted his vote. When the district court upheld the Hanna amendment, declaring that geographic area seemed as legitimate as population in establishing voting districts, Nolan appealed to the United States Supreme Court. In 1962, the high court addressed the issues involved in Nolan's case when it decreed in *Baker v Carr* that the states must apportion seats not by "land or trees or pastures," but as closely as possible by the principle of "one person, one vote."

The Supreme Court remanded the Nolan case back to the Federal District Court for rehearing under the guidelines of the *Baker v Carr* decision. Throughout these developments the Ohio AFL-CIO's legal staff, now headed by David Clayman, provided the courts with briefs supportive of Nolan's position. It was jubilant, therefore, when in October 1964, the district court held the Hanna amendment unconstitutional and directed that a reapportionment plan in line with the Supreme Court's ruling be drafted for ratification by popular vote "by the next regular session of the General Assembly."

Political maneuvering now took over. In November 1964, as we have seen, Ohio voters pared back the Republican party's majority in the Ohio House and sent an equal number of Democrats and Republicans to the Senate. Governor Rhodes quickly realized that any reapportionment plan devised by the upcoming 106th General Assembly would have a more bipartisan focus than one created by the current Republican dominated Legislature, and so he hurriedly summoned the 105th

General Assembly back into emergency session just weeks before its term expired. Out of the GOP-controlled lame duck session emerged what came to be known as Issue 3, a reapportionment plan designed to minimize the effect of the "one man, one vote" ruling on the smaller counties, the traditional source of Republican and conservative strength in the Ohio Legislature. Since apportionment involved amending the state's constitution, Issue 3 was scheduled to appear on the ballot in the May 1965 elections.

The Republicans hoped to gain voter approval for their reapportionment scheme by packaging it with three other ballot issues popular with various segments of the population. "VOTE YES ON ALL FOUR — NO INCREASE IN TAXES," was Governor Rhodes' snappy slogan. Initially Rhodes and the GOP simply did not believe that the issue would encounter rough sledding and was taken by surprise when the Ohio AFL-CIO's campaign to defeat it gained steam. The sponsors did not start raising an Issue 3 "kitty" until late in March 1965, and did not form the Ohio Home Rule Committee to concentrate on just Issue 3 until a month before the election. But when the supporters did mobilize their forces, they commanded a more powerful army than labor had even faced during its 1958 right-to-work battle. Issue 3 had the backing of every major paper in the state except those in Dayton which did not oppose it, but were not frantically trying to ram it down readers' throats. Eight TV stations endorsed it and only one stood against. Issue 3 also had the backing of all the major business associations, including the Ohio Information Committee, Ohio Chamber of Commerce, Ohio Manufacturers' Association, Ohio Farm Bureau, Ohio Bankers Association, and Ohio State Council of Retail Merchants. The pressures were so intense that the Ohio League of Women Voters violated past policies by issuing an endorsement, and the Cincinnati Charter Party also came out for it. Dr. Robert E. Tschanty, President of the Ohio State Medical Association, sent a letter to members stating that "If Issue 3 does not pass, reapportionment will be dictated by a Federal Court, and medicine may never again have a friendly State legislature." The state universities initially plugged "All 4" fearing that the building program promised them in the $290-million Issue 2 would be jeopardized by a "Vote No" trend. Governor Rhodes threw an unprecedented amount of state resources into the campaign. He reportedly siphoned off nearly a million dollars into literature designed to lay a base for the proponent's campaign. Rhodes also kept the state's airplane busy on his personal hedgehopping tour of Ohio towns plugging the issue and commanded the GOP machinery, his cabinet, and thousands of state employees to back the effort. "THE POWER STRUCTURE OF OHIO COMMITTED ITSELF TO THIS ISSUE TO A MUCH GREATER EXTENT THAN IT DID TO THE 'RIGHT-TO-WORK' AMENDMENT IN 1958" declared a confidential post-election report prepared by the Burr Communication Agency for the Ohio AFL-CIO Executive Board.

That same report by the Burr Agency also provided a detailed analysis on how labor defeated this coalition. "The single most significant development was the Ohio AFL-CIO board meeting last January (1965) where, meeting with COPE Representative Walter Davis, the Ohio AFL-CIO agreed to make the effort. Everything that followed flowed from this decision." The report praised labor for its willingness to spend the money needed to do the job. "When funds were slow coming in,

Labor kept its confidence. The program moved forward because those responsible had the faith." The Burr Agency also thought that the labor movement made a wise move when it returned to many of the strategies that had proved successful in 1958, particularly re-establishing United Organized Labor of Ohio and forging alliances with a number of prominent professors, attorneys, businessmen, and civil rights leaders. In the fight over Issue 3, labor took the lead over the weak and disorganized Ohio Democratic Party, and in the process gave the politicos heart. Moreover, the Ohio AFL-CIO engaged in an aggressive public relations and advertising program. Whereas the supporters of Issue 3 relied on newspapers, labor understood the driving public's radio habit and aired 6,000 radio spots during the final two weeks of the campaign.

In the final analysis, however, the Burr report saw the willingness to concentrate only on the one issue and to educate seriously the public on the complexities of apportionment as the most important ingredients in the Ohio AFL-CIO recipe to victory over Issue 3. The labor movement and its allies won the war of facts and credibility, convincing the voting public that it was waging the struggle to advance democracy and not self-interest. "After much soul searching, the decision was reached to 'go the hard way,' explaining enough of the complex issue so that people would know why it was bad. This involved an enormous amount of research, and a great deal of localized material showing how specific areas would be affected. Without this effort," the Burr Agency concluded, "we are convinced we could not possibly have pulled off such 'surprises' as defeating the issue 3 to 2 in normally Republican Counties like Allen (Lima), Clark (Springfield), Stark (Canton), and Fairfield, or defeating the issue by three thousand votes in Franklin County."

The successful campaign against Issue 3 gave organized labor in Ohio what some pundits believed was an even greater victory than its defeat of the right-to-work amendment in 1958. "The victory belongs wholly and entirely to Ohio labor," Esther Murray of the national Women's Activities Division told Robert Bollard. "This is one nobody can swipe from you, or underrate." Not only were labor's opponents even more powerful, active, and affluent than in 1958, but the stakes of the game were higher. "Issue 3 was more than just an effort (by Republicans) to keep control," the Burr report concluded. "If Issue 3 had passed and survived Federal Court tests, Ohio would have been even more in the grip of one party than it has ever been in the past."

While successful in defeating a bad reapportionment plan, the Spring 1965 victory did not guarantee that a good plan would be established. During the following Summer, the State Apportionment Board made up of Governor Rhodes, State Auditor Roger Cloud, and Secretary of State Ted Brown, all Republicans, devised a new plan that gave them extensive discretion in drawing districts and allowed a twenty percent population differential between the largest and smallest districts. With great audacity, they simply declared that the plan replaced various provisions of the state's constitution and would be law. On behalf of the Ohio AFL-CIO, Frank King immediately challenged the Apportionment Board's plan in the Federal District Court, only to have the court rule in October that the Board's plan would suffice for the November elections in 1966, but then would need to be submitted to the voters for final approval.

When the plan was finally presented to the voters as Issue 2 in the Spring of 1967 the Ohio AFL-CIO again waged a successful campaign to defeat it. And again the Republican-controlled Apportionment Board set to work devising yet a new plan for the fall elections, but this time paying greater attention to some to the criticism of earlier apportionment schemes. In the November 1967 election, reapportionment took the name of Issue 1 on the ballot, and despite continued objections by the Ohio AFL-CIO, voters finally passed the plan. While the final apportionment scheme was not what labor would have preferred, nonetheless it was a significant improvement over the two previous plans submitted to the voters. "In summary then," the *Officer's Report* for 1968 noted, "Labor did achieve a measure of success because the present reapportionment plan is much better than the original proposal. But it's still not good enough."

VI

While the Ohio AFL-CIO enjoyed a major victory in defeating Issue 3, that accomplishment did not lead to an extended era of political strength. On the contrary, for the next three years, organized labor's successes at the polls and with the General Assembly were few and far between. As mentioned above, the final reapportionment plan approved by the voters in November 1967 fell short of labor's goal of having representation based solely on population. Even more disappointing were the results of the November 1966 election in which the Ohio AFL-CIO's endorsed candidate for Governor, State Senator Frazier Reams, put up a poor showing against Rhodes. "Labor," *News and Views* had to admit, "suffered a political setback." Not only was Rhodes re-elected, but the GOP increased its majority in both the House and the Senate. As a consequence, according to Frank King, throughout the 107th General Assembly "the Ohio AFL-CIO scurried around from chamber to chamber keeping holes plugged in the dike containing scores of anti-worker, anti-people legislation. Despite our efforts some bills were signed into law which hit directly at our members." Foremost among such measures was the "tax-education bill" which sought to bail out the state's failing education system by increasing the sales tax to four cents and adding various commodities including beer and cigarettes to the taxable item list. The one bright spot in the political picture came in the Spring of 1967 when the Ohio AFL-CIO and the Ohio Democratic Party worked together to defeat Governor Rhodes' Ohio Bond Commission plan which would have taken away from the voter the right to approve or disapprove future state indebtedness.

The Ohio AFL-CIO's inability to sustain the momentum started by Lyndon Johnson's November 1964 re-election and the May 1965 victory over the Republican reapportionment plan festered discord in the Columbus headquarters between President King and Secretary-Treasurer Bollard. Like Elmer Cope before him, Bob Bollard believed that the merger convention had intended the Secretary-Treasurer to be the dominant figure within the organization. But when the delegates to the 1964 convention elected Frank King as President they also changed the constitution to make it clear that he was to be the primary spokesperson for the organization in political affairs. Increasingly, the two men found themselves clashing over jurisdiction and inevitably brought the Executive Board into the fray. In addressing the competing roles of the President and Secretary-Treasurer, the Executive Board revealed how far the state body had progressed from the old tensions between the AFL and the CIO at the time of the merger. Leading the drive to make Frank King, a former AFL Bricklayer, the top officer of the organization were the two mainstays of the CIO, the UAW and the Steelworkers, Secretary-Treasurer Bollard's own organization.

In October 1965, the Board took the first steps to resolve the problems arising from having a dual leadership structure. In the past the Secretary-Treasurer had represented the state office at conventions of the national AFL-CIO and the President had carried credentials from his international union. But now the Board ruled that the President should be its sole delegate, a decision that did not sit well with Bollard. A further clarification of the roles of the President and Secretary-Treasurer occurred at the June 1966 Ohio AFL-CIO convention when the delegates amended the constitution again, this time defining the President as the top executive officer and changing the secretary-treasurership from a decision-making to an administrative post. While this action clarified lines of authority and communication, it naturally displeased Bollard. Recognizing that his role in the organization had changed, on January 6, 1967, he resigned his office and went to work in the Washington, D.C., office of the American Federation of State, County, and Municipal Employees.

For the second time in five years the Ohio AFL-CIO Executive Board found itself having to elect a Secretary-Treasurer to finish out a term. Following Frank King's recommendation, on January 27, 1967, the Board elevated Warren J Smith from his staff position to the vacancy. Born in 1932, Smith was a native of Lima and a graduate of The Ohio State University and The Ohio State

University Law School. Smith had worked at Superior Coach Company in Lima and then served a stint in the U.S. Army. In 1955, while still a law student, he went to work part-time for the Ohio CIO Council. In 1959, the same year he passed the bar exam, he became assistant to Elmer Cope, and then in 1961 he assumed the duties of legislative representative. Smith was a quiet, temperate man, a strategist, a person always on top of his facts, yet someone not inclined to seek the limelight. Preferring to work in the background, during his long tenure as Secretary-Treasurer, Smith seldom orated before convention delegates or sought to capture newspaper headlines. Yet for the next nineteen years, he was the guiding force within the organization.

With Warren Smith's appointment as Secretary-Treasurer, the Ohio AFL-CIO commenced a period of internal stability after a five-year spree of democratic turmoil which saw the presidency, secretary-treasurership, and several Executive Board seats change occupants several times. At a period of time when the courts and Congress were exposing corruption and tyranny in a handful of unions, the Ohio AFL-CIO proved itself a vehicle for the democratic desires of its members. It successfully embraced the accouterments of democracy — politics, debate, conflict, and contest for office — within a framework in which all parties—winners or losers —accepted the principles of fair play, majority rule, and respect for the minority. For the next several years, at least, the organization de-emphasized internal politics and focused on the task of representing labor in the broader arena of state affairs.

Chapter Four

Spirit and Spite, 1968-1974

I

In the decade after the merger convention of the Ohio AFL-CIO, dramatic changes occurred in almost every area of American life. By the late 1960s, people looked and dressed differently, with longer hair and more casual attire. Cars too had lost their flamboyant tailfins, with smaller models gaining popularity, including VW Beetles and other imports. And increasingly America was younger, as the first wave of baby boomers, children born in the aftermath of World War II, gained adulthood, joined the workforce, or swelled college classrooms. Whereas their parents and grandparents, products of the Depression era, had struggled hard to advance from bib-overalls to gray flannel suits, youth of both genders in the late 1960s considered T-shirts and blue jeans a fashion statement. In music, the British Beatles dominated the airways with their psychedelic *Sgt. Pepper's Lonely Hearts Club Band,* which included the cryptic song "Lucy in the Sky with Diamonds" about the drug LSD. While only a minority of youth actually lived an alternative lifestyle in rural communes or in San Francisco's Haight Ashbury, their counter culture values intruded everyday life through TV, movies, and rock music. Everyone could relate to folksinger Bob Dylan's wail: "For the times 'they are a-changin'!"

Above all, Americans had become more political than they had been in the 1950s when President Dwight Eisenhower praised the United States as the land of consensus and continuity. Television forced everyone to confront the struggle for civil rights, urban riots, campus unrest, and the war in Vietnam, and each person reacted differently. Even as President Lyndon Johnson boldly advanced New Deal-like programs including Medicare, Headstart, and a war on poverty, liberalism came under assault. The 1964 presidential campaigns of both Barry Goldwater and George Wallace, while failing, nonetheless recruited supporters to right-wing causes. Concomitantly, a youth-oriented New Left condemned established liberals for practicing imperialism abroad and imposing bureaucracy and conformity at home. Thus, whereas editorialists had formerly complained about the complacency of the 1950s, now they observed how everyone seemed to have an opinion on current affairs, even if they did not exercise their right to vote.

II

The 1960s spirit of change also gripped the Ohio AFL-CIO as new personalities instilled a new sense of mission in the organization. A decade after its founding, a surprisingly large number of the founding fathers had left the scene. Neither President Frank King nor Secretary-Treasurer Warren Smith had been delegates to the merger convention (although both had been in attendance, the former as a guest and the latter as a staff person). Likewise, only four Vice Presidents remained of the original twenty-four member Executive Board. The office staff had also experienced significant turn over, with just Warren Pate, George DeNucci, Jane Adams (Ely), and Ira Thompson remaining at their posts. Indeed, in the Summer of 1967 an internal restructuring occurred with Richard Sears taking over Education and Research Programs, Charles "Chuck" Borsari becoming Public Relations Director, Charles Mix serving as head of Community Services, and Frank Bezon assuming the post of Compensation Director. Even the organization's logo underwent an overhaul. Out went the two clasped hands within the outline of Ohio and in came a striking contrast of mosaic tiles and three modernist figures of workers marching forward "United in Purpose." Among officers and staff alike, a feeling prevailed that the moment had arrived to transform the Ohio AFL-CIO from a defensive organization with episodic success like in 1958 and 1965, to an aggressive, pro-active force continually shaping the state's political destiny.

In May 1967, victories on significant ballot issues fueled such optimism. As mentioned in the last chapter, for a second time the Ohio AFL-CIO successfully educated voters about the pitfalls of a Republican apportionment scheme and led its defeat. The Ohio AFL-CIO also successfully spearheaded a coalition consisting of the Democratic party, farmer organizations, fraternal societies, and civic groups in thwarting Governor Rhodes' pet scheme to create an Ohio Bond Commission (OBC). The Ohio AFL-CIO was not opposed in principle to financing internal improvements through bonds, taking each proposal up on its merits. But in this case it objected to removing from the people the power to vote on individual bond issues and placing that authority in a non-elected board. Defeat of the Ohio Bond Commission constituted a major setback for Rhodes, who had declared the proposed amendment "the most important piece of legislation I've ever known of since I've been in public life." Having gone all out for its passage, Rhodes, according to reporter Richard G. Zimmerman, "never quite got over the loss of his OBC proposal. His confidence in his own political infallibility seemed shaken."

Even prior to the May 1967 victories over the second Republican reapportionment scheme and Rhodes' Ohio Bond Commission, the officers and staff had commenced laying the foundation for a more concerted political action program. In the Spring of 1967, the Ohio AFL-CIO commissioned the "Kraft Poll" which developed a statistical profile of Ohio unionists and asked union members what were the most important issues of the day. "The results in some cases were astonishing," Chuck Borsari reported. "We learned our average member wasn't overly concerned about workmen's compensation, minimum wage, unemployment compensation, situs picketing, or even repeal of 14-B of the infamous Taft-Hartley law. Instead, this average member was concerned about his property tax bill, the condition of his local schools, whether his garbage was picked up on schedule, air and water pollution, and — of course — sky rocketing auto insurance premiums and the growing menace of mass cancellation by auto insurance companies." The officers of the Ohio AFL-CIO took the insights from the Kraft Poll seriously. While the state body did not lessen its legislative and legal work on compensation programs or other traditional issues, it did more aggressively pursue the concerns identified by its members. As a result of the Kraft Poll, then, the legislative agenda of the Ohio AFL-CIO broadened from the late 1960s onward.

On March 31, 1967, the Executive Board attempted to rejuvenate labor's political presence when it approved a new political strategy. Entitled *The Spirit of '67*, the program had three main features. First and foremost, the plan called for employing the emerging technology of computers and "data processing" to develop a statewide list of union members, complete with the member's name, address, telephone number, voting precinct, ward, and party preference. In the past, the old file cards developed by the Women's Activities Department at best contained only ten per cent of the state's union members. Now with computers the potential existed to locate all but a small fraction.

Second, with such a computerized list, the Ohio AFL-CIO planned to reach out to each member with vital information to inform his or her political choices. In the past, the state body relied on the inadequate and biased coverage of city newspapers, often opposed to labor's stance, to present its case. With the assistance of a computerized list, labor leaders could now communicate views on legislation, candidates, and social issues directly to each of the state body's 800,000 members through a high quality, monthly publication to be called *Focus*.

The third component of *The Spirit of '67* involved assisting city and county central bodies in their political work. On the one hand, the Columbus headquarters would provide local affiliates with computer lists that identified by ward, precinct, party preference, and household each union member in the district. The locals could then target mailings and phone the homes of union members in order to mobilize support in local campaigns.

On the other hand, the state body planned to send a portion of the program's per capita tax increase back to the central bodies to help finance critical local elections.

Having witnessed the defeat of *Blueprint for Victory* in 1962, Warren Smith and Frank King were determined not to have *The Spirit of '67* suffer the same fate. They worked hard to avert the divisions that occurred in 1962 and secured the united support of the Executive Board. They also spent the summer taking a "road show" around the state, holding Saturday morning meetings to explain the plan to anyone who was interested. At these sessions, Warren Smith presented the technical details of the plan, while Frank King discussed its broader importance. "*The Spirit of '67*," King drove home, "will enable the Ohio AFL-CIO to conduct a continuing political action program instead of the crisis-to-crisis efforts we have put forth in the past." Unlike Morris Riger five years before, Smith and King were up front about the cost of the plan, a five cents increase in per capital tax. By being realistic about costs and providing members with information on both how the increase would be spent and how Ohio's per capita payments compared with those of other state central bodies, the leaders won begrudging acceptance for the program from the membership. And finally, to ensure the program was in place for the 1968 primaries and to guard against other issues undermining its fate, Frank King called a special Constitutional Convention on October 6, 1967, solely to approve *The Spirit of '67* and the required per capita tax increase.

Once the delegates officially approved the program at the October special convention, the state office lost no time in activating it. The Ohio AFL-CIO set up a centralized workshop to process the membership lists of participating international unions, employing thirty-four girls from Columbus' Bishop Ready High School. For weeks on end, the girls worked every day after school from 3:30 until 7:00 pm and on Saturdays from 9:00 to 5:00 compiling data about individuals to be key-punched on data processing cards. Given the immensity of the task, the state body wisely elected to enter first information on union members who lived in the ten largest metropolitan areas of the state so it could be used in the spring primaries. While the high school girls worked away, the state officers held five meetings with Central Labor Councils to explain the Councils' role in the program. Beginning in January 1968, the Ohio AFL-CIO's Public Relations Department augmented its weekly newsletter, *News and Views*, with the monthly magazine *Focus*. Whereas *News and Views* had for years been sent to a few thousand officers and staff persons within the Ohio labor movement, *Focus* went into the living room of hundreds of thousands of rank-and-file members and friends. Each month it explored in depth a particular issue and soon gained recognition as the nation's best state labor magazine.

III

The first test for *The Spirit of '67* came with the Spring 1968 primaries when the Ohio AFL-CIO led the campaign to deny incumbent U.S. Senator Frank J. Lausche renomination. For years Lausche was a thorn in the side of labor and an embarrassment to the state's Democratic Party. As both Governor and then as Senator, Lausche opposed almost every program labor endorsed. In 1958, for example, he came out in favor of the right-to-work amendment, and in 1965 he had backed Senator

Everett Dirksen's filibuster to block repeal of Section 14(b) of the Taft-Hartley Act. A *Congressional Quarterly* survey in the early 1960s reported that as a U.S. Senator Lausche voted sixty-seven percent of the time with the Republicans and a mere twenty-seven percent with his own party. Only Strom Thurmond among the Democrats voted more often with the GOP (and he at least had the integrity eventually to switch parties). Both the national and state AFL-CIO leadership desperately wanted Lausche out of office, but for years they felt paralyzed to act because of the disarray within the Ohio Democratic Party.

This condition, however, began to change in 1966 when the Democrats' candidate for Governor, Frazier Reams, selected fellow Toledoan Morton Neipp as the new state party chairman, and Neipp in turn appointed Cleveland political leader Pete O'Grady as the party's Executive Director to run the Columbus office. Both men were determined to build a stronger and more united state party and recognized that this could not be accomplished as long as Lausche blatantly undermined the Democrats' platform and candidates. In the Spring of 1967, Frank King, Warren Smith, various leaders from the Steelworkers and United Automobile Workers, and Al Barkan from the national AFL-CIO Committee on Political Education solidified plans to challenge Lausche in the 1968 primary. To run against him they recruited John J. Gilligan, a liberal who had long supported labor while a member of the Cincinnati City Council and during his one term in the U.S. House of Representatives. Educated, ambitious, and, in 1967, out of work as a politician with his opportunities significantly stymied in Republican-dominated Cincinnati, Gilligan's only true hope for a political future lay at the state level. To protect himself against charges of disloyalty, Gilligan agreed to run against Lausche only if the Ohio Democratic Party State Central Committee broke tradition and endorsed him, which in an unprecedented move it did.

By the time Gilligan launched his primary campaign in mid-January 1968, the Ohio AFL-CIO had executed much of *The Spirit of '67*. The Bishop Ready students had computerized information on seventy per cent of the state's union membership and this information was shocking: six out of ten unionists in Ohio were not registered to vote. But unlike in the past, now the leaders of the Ohio AFL-CIO and the city and county central bodies knew exactly who those people were and how to contact them. As a result of a massive drive, 85,000 new voters registered.

When the four hundred members of the Ohio Committee on Political Education met on February 21, 1968, they abstained from endorsing any specific candidate in the presidential primary and instead placed their undivided resources behind Gilligan. The state body literally drained its treasury to fund the campaign and the national AFL-CIO COPE also sent more money into Ohio to aid Gilligan than to any other state. A large part of the funds paid for extensive television advertising since none of the large newspapers in the state endorsed Gilligan. But considerable expense also occurred when the Ohio AFL-CIO Public Relations Department utilized the computerized list to mail special regional issues of *Focus*, as well as a twenty-four-page pamphlet comparing Lausche and Gilligan, to hundreds of thousands of unionist throughout the state.

The unified attack by the Ohio AFL-CIO, the state's Democratic Party, and the Gilligan campaign team took an overconfident Lausche by surprise. The Gilligan forces out campaigned and out spent Lausche by a five-to-one margin. And the effort paid off. The almost one million Democrats who voted on May 7 gave Gilligan fifty-five per cent of their votes over forty-five per cent to the incumbent Senator. Gilligan carried nine of the state's ten largest counties, the places where the labor movement had most fully implemented *The Spirit of '67*. "Results in key areas . . ." observed an internal assessment made for the Executive Board, "suggest that the computer program was the major factor in COPE-endorsed John Gilligan's stunning 135,000-vote victory over Sen. Frank Lausche ... The computer program permitted the most effective labor precinct organization yet, and the people-to-people campaign paid off."

Yet, even while the state's leadership proclaimed Gilligan's primary victory as the first ray of sunshine in a bright political future, ominous clouds appeared on the horizon. Early in 1968, UAW President Walter Ruether, who had numerous personal disagreements with AFL-CIO chief George Meany, broke with the national federation over various foreign policy issues, including U.S. involvement in the Vietnam War. The subsequent departure of UAW locals from the Ohio AFL-CIO left *The Spirit of '67* program in shambles. "In Ohio," Public Relations Director Chuck Borsari noted, "the UAW made up about 25% of all paid affiliations to the Ohio AFL-CIO. Consequently, the withdrawal of the UAW from our organization deprived the Ohio AFL-CIO of one-fourth of our operating income . . . . Cuts were made . . . in several key areas. Amounts of money the Ohio AFL-CIO was prepared to return to local Central Labor Councils to help support their programs was reduced to near zero. So was the amount of funds available for contributions to state legislative candidates."

Still, the state's leadership worked valiantly to save the core of *The Spirit of '67* — the computerized registry of state union members and *Focus* as a means of directly communicating to them. The financial pinch caused by the UAW's departure would not be relieved until the June 1970 Convention when the delegates agreed to another five cents increase in the per capita tax for a total of fifteen cents. In the meanwhile, instead of expanding personnel as called for in *The Spirit of '67*, Columbus headquarters worked with two less staff and two less secretaries by November 1968 than it had in 1966. With the General Assembly now meeting annually, instead of biannually, the Columbus office registered each staff member as a lobbyist. Headquarters kept old equipment running rather than modernize, tapped money put on reserve for staff pensions to pay bills, borrowed $50,000 from the Steelworkers, and got the national COPE to underwrite much of the $70,000 annually needed to keep the computer lists updated.

In the end, forces far beyond labor's control determined the outcome of the November 1968 elections. Republican presidential candidate Richard Nixon hit a popular chord in promising to promote "law and order" while cracking down on pot, pornography, protests, and permissiveness. More subtly he played the race card with his Southern strategy and turned the once solidly Democratic South into a conservative Republican stronghold. Hubert Humphrey, on the other hand, was burdened by George Wallace's independent appeal for working class votes, Johnson's Vietnam War policies, and the vivid scenes of rioting at the 1968 Democratic National Convention in Chicago. Given the intensity of feelings at the time, it is doubtful that the outcome of the election would have been different even had the labor movement not split apart. The Republicans carried Ohio for Nixon, guaranteed their party's control of both houses of the upcoming General Assembly, and sent William Saxbe over John Gilligan to the U.S. Senate.

Frank King and Warren Smith were disappointed but not disheartened by the election results. "We believe our program — bobtailed as it is from lack of funds — is just beginning," they told delegates at the 1970 Ohio AFL-CIO convention. Believing that they had found a formula in *The Spirit of '67* that would produce greater electoral success, they regrouped to fight another day. Within a few months of the convention their hard work to keep the spirit alive would pay off. And throughout the 1970s, the computerized program developed in 1967 would make the Ohio AFL-CIO one of the most effective political forces in the state. It might not always win elections, but even when not victorious, the margin of defeat would be greatly reduced. *Focus*, moreover, proved a singular asset to the Federation. Within a year of its first issue the magazine received honors and awards for both its layout and its substance, including several International Labor Press Association "Award of Merit." No other state federation, and few international unions, matched the Ohio AFL-CIO in its ability to inform so many people in such a professional manner. Equally important, readership surveys conducted by The Ohio State University's Labor Education and Research Service showed that *Focus* stimulated a significant change in membership attitudes on critical issues facing working people.

IV

While *The Spirit of '67*, despite setbacks, proved

successful, another initiative from the late 1960s crashed — the Ohio AFL-CIO's proposed automobile insurance company, Unity of Ohio. Back in 1945 the powerful insurance industry successfully lobbied the U.S. Congress to exempt them from federal anti-trust laws if the states regulated the industry. The companies then descended on various states, including Ohio, and persuaded lawmakers to enact one-sided legislation that posed as regulation. The Ohio law, for instance, basically made the state's Insurance Department a filing office with no authority in establishing rates. With virtually no restrictions on them, auto insurance companies dramatically boosted premiums in the state during the mid-1960s. From September 1965 through November 1966, the average cost of liability insurance jumped 17.9 percent statewide. Yet, during that same period the actual underwriting costs of auto insurance dropped 4.1 percent nationally.

While many people complained about the climbing rates, the Ohio AFL-CIO was one of the few groups to do anything about it. At an emergency meeting on December 5, 1966, the Executive Board joined with the Academy of Trial Lawyers to challenge the increases through administrative channels and in court. In May 1967, however, Ohio Insurance Superintendent William Morris rejected the Ohio AFL-CIO's appeal, claiming that the rates were neither excessive nor unfairly discriminatory. When the state body next turned to the Court of Common Pleas for redress, the judge ruled that only insurance companies, and not individuals or groups representing individuals, could appeal decisions of the Insurance Superintendent under Ohio law. Two years later, the Ohio Supreme Court would affirm the lower court's ruling.

The decision forced the Ohio AFL-CIO to refocus its energies toward changing the law through the Ohio General Assembly. In September 1967 Frank King, Warren Smith, and a group of sympathetic state legislators proposed a "Twentieth Century Bill of Rights" to protect Ohioans from "wheeling and dealing insurance companies." They proposed to require the Superintendent of Insurance to approve or reject rate changes before they were implemented and to make all decisions of the Superintendent of Insurance appealable by consumers. Despite strong public support of labor's "Twentieth Century Bill of Rights," the insurance industry worked closely with the Republican-controlled General Assembly to block any reform legislation from coming to a vote.

The failure of the reform proposal to gain even a hearing in the Legislature forced the Ohio AFL-CIO to search for another remedy. They decided to create a union-owned insurance company. The idea of such a company was creative but not that far-fetched. Living in Columbus, the leaders of the Ohio AFL-CIO knew the story of how in the 1920s a small group of farmers combined to form what today is Nationwide Insurance. They were also aware that in the late 1950s, a band of teachers created Educators and Executives (E&E) Insurance, which was later taken over by J.C. Penney. And finally they could look at the example of various credit unions forming their own insurance outlets, like Michigan League General Insurance Company, to whom the Ohio AFL-CIO would turn to for professional assistance in setting up its own company.

On September 15 and 16, 1969, the Executive Board reviewed a proposal for a labor-owned auto insurance firm and authorized the officers to negotiate contracts and establish a company. Final approval to establish the company, called Unity of Ohio, was given by the delegates to the 1970 state convention. The company would be totally owned by union members and their locals and central bodies and would sell policies only to members and their families. Under Ohio law, an insurance company needed one dollar in reserve for every three dollars of insurance it sold. The leaders of the Ohio AFL-CIO, who were to be the officers of Unity of Ohio, projected that before Unity could start selling insurance policies, therefore, it needed to develop a reserve of $5,000,000 through the sale of stock at ten dollars a share. The officers placed the price per share as low as possible to encourage widespread participation by unionists in the state. If every member in the state bought just one share, the company would be in incredible shape. If only five percent of the membership participated, along with the 2,000 local unions in the state, the company could still operate.

The sale of stocks began with a bang but ended in a whimper. On August 1, 1971, sales commenced with a surge of purchases by those deeply interested in the project. Unity reached its goal of $1,500,000 by January 1972, but from that point on sales slowed down. The first signs that the venture faced problems came in April 1972, when Secretary-Treasurer Warren Smith reported that Unity had sold $2,000,000 in stock but that purchases lagged behind anticipation, with fewer than half of the local affiliates and still less than one percent of the state unionists investing. The picture did not look any brighter by the time of the June convention, at which time the delegates decided to place a January 1, 1973, deadline for the sale of $4,000,000 in stock. When the targeted date arrived, stock totaled only $2,404,180. This came from 9,475 individual union members and 968 local unions. With only one dissenting vote, the Executive Board on January 25, 1973, voted to end the efforts to establish the nation's first wholly-owned union automobile insurance company for lack of interest and to return all money to investors. Unity died at birth without ever issuing a policy.

V

The Ohio AFL-CIO recognized the November 1970 election as exceptionally important because of the new reapportionment process. As *Focus* informed its readership: "Ohio officials will establish new Legislative and Congressional districts after the results of the 1970 census are revealed. This will involve considerable juggling (gerrymandering) of district boundaries. Power to draw new boundaries will rest with five individuals — the Governor, Auditor, Secretary of State, and the Republican and Democratic leaders of the Legislature. The last time this event took place, the Republicans controlled the Apportionment Board. They have ruled Ohio ever since."

Since 1967,the state officers had prepared for the 1970 election, primarily by refining *The Spirit of '67* so that precinct finders were available for most of the larger urban counties. Using this data, city and county central bodies conducted extensive registration efforts which changed the ratio of union members signed up to vote from four-in-ten in 1967 to six-in-ten by the 1970 election. Moreover, after only a year in existence, *Focus* had evolved into an incredibly polished and refined informational tool. During the early months of 1970, it educated its 800,000-plus readers on the issues of the day, including an award-winning exposé "Why Ohio Schools Are Closing." Finally, while the United Automobile Workers remained outside of the state body, the two organizations had developed a constructive working relationship on legislative and electoral programs. For the most part, they pulled in the same political direction, although not always on the same rope.

Fortunately, the political winds in 1970 blew in a Democratic direction. The Ohio Constitution barred popular James Rhodes from seeking a third term, forcing the GOP to turn to the bland former Speaker of the Ohio House, Roger W. Cloud. "To know Roger Cloud is to forget Roger Cloud," his press secretary even admitted. The Republicans also had to account for the state's poor financial condition, widespread school closings for lack of funds, the simultaneous existence of inflation and high unemployment, a series of environmental crises, and a scandal involving Rhodes that made the front pages of *Life* magazine. The state Democrats, on the other hand, united behind the energetic candidacy of John J. Gilligan, who already had widespread voter recognition because of his 1968 senatorial campaign.

On November 3, a massive "get out the vote" drive paid off as four out of six labor-endorsed statewide candidates won — John Gilligan for Governor, William Brown for Attorney General, Joseph Ferguson for Auditor, and Gertrude Donahey as the state's first female Treasurer. These victories guaranteed that the next reapportionment of the state would correct some gross inequities. Yet the 1970 election to the General Assembly was still apportioned under the old Republican scheme, resulting in GOP majorities in both houses. Even though

Democrats collected 51.9 percent of the vote for the Ohio House, they only won 45 percent of the seats. As the Republicans retained control of the 109th General Assembly, the outlook for labor's legislative program remained questionable. Even after a new apportionment plan went into effect in 1972, the Republicans controlled the Senate by one vote, although the Democrats would began a twenty-year reign in the House.

VI

Few Ohioans could doubt what the first major issue would be for the new Governor and General Assembly to tackle. After eight years of Rhodes' policies of low taxes and minimal social services, few informed citizens could dodge the fact that the state government simply lacked the funds to provide even the minimum functions it had been providing. While in 1968 Ohio ranked fifteenth in the nation for per capita personal income, it stood forty-sixth in expenditures for education, forty-ninth for health and hospitals, fortieth for welfare, and forty-third in protecting natural resources. As a low tax state, in 1968 Ohio ranked forty-ninth in total per capita tax revenues, with the logical corollary that it was also forty-ninth in per capita expenditures for all state services. The government of Ohio simply did less with less and was on the verge of doing nothing at all. With the state's share of funding for K-12 education dropping from forty percent to twenty-nine percent during Rhodes' administration, a dozen school systems by 1969 had to close for varying periods because of a lack of money. Likewise, outside evaluators found Ohio's mental hospitals to be little more than prisons.

During his gubernatorial campaign, Gilligan had candidly announced his intent to seek a new state income tax. Ohio was the only major industrial state without one. Shortly after Gilligan was elected he established a Citizens' Task Force on Tax Reform headed by Jacob Davis, Chairman of the Kroger Company, to work out the details.

While members of the Ohio AFL-CIO served on the Governor's Task Force, the organization opposed any new method of taxation until the current tax system was reformed "to 'balance' that tax load between the workers of Ohio and those for whom we work." As a State Senator until January 1969, Frank King had long sought to close loopholes through which Buckeye businesses dodged a fair share of the state's tax burden. Now, with a change in taxation imminent, he saw an opportunity to act. With the cooperation of the United Automobile Workers, the Ohio AFL-CIO created the Tax Reform Action Committee (TRAC) to push for increasing state revenues through reform of the current tax system. It contended that special tax advantages or omissions in the current tax laws needed to be corrected before Ohio introduced a new state tax. The state could raise an additional $500 million dollars, the Tax Reform Action Committee argued, by plugging loopholes in the sales tax and by placing taxes on corporate profits, the use of natural resources, insurance companies, nationally chartered banks, and commercial vehicles. The Tax Reform Action Committee correctly predicted that if the state adopted the income tax system without first making these corrections, in all probability they would never be made.

Throughout 1971 a "battle of the budget" preoccupied the Ohio Legislature. Governor Gilligan pushed one tax plan, the Ohio AFL-CIO and the UAW advocated a second, and factions within the Republican majority in the General Assembly either totally opposed an increase or sought to obtain the needed increase in state revenue through raising the sales tax. Recognizing the difficulty of working through regular legislative channels, the Tax Reform Action Committee boldly decided to mobilize widespread public backing for its plan and to use Ohio's initiative process to compel the Legislature to consider its proposal. To this end, union volunteers collected over 100,000 signatures of qualified voters, yet the General Assembly only gave labor's tax plan a perfunctory hearing.

In the end, the more responsible business interests in the state conceded that Ohio needed more revenue to improve services. They also recognized that Gilligan's income tax posed less of a threat to their interests than did the proposal advanced by the Tax Reform Action Committee. Likewise, the Ohio AFL-CIO acknowledged that its plan had little chance of passage in the Republican-controlled General Assembly. The unions also bitterly opposed a sales tax increase as advocated by many in the GOP. Putting realism above idealism, the Ohio AFL-CIO consequently agreed to go along with Gilligan's tax on income and corporate profits as the best solution obtainable to the crisis.

On January 1, 1972, Ohio became the forty-fifth state in the nation to levy a tax on the incomes of individuals and corporate profits. Yet the battle over the new tax had not ended, for a group of die-hard conservatives successfully petitioned to have a referendum on the income tax placed on the November 1972 ballot. The Ohio AFL-CIO joined a wide coalition to stop this move. "We've been around the Ohio Legislature a long time,"

Focus informed its readership, "And given the history of taxation enactment by the Legislature, we know the alternative to the present income tax will be worse — much worse — for most of our Union members." Through a concerted educational campaign, the move to repeal the income tax was defeated by a substantial margin. "For many years to come," historian George W. Knepper observed, "the state sales tax would remain Ohio's largest source of state revenue, but by the mid-1980s the general revenue fund was receiving more money from the income tax than from the sales tax. Despite cries that Ohio had become a high-tax state, comparative figures showed that it still ranked well below the national average in the level of state and local taxes paid by its citizens."

VII

The compromising that resulted in the passage of the 1971 income tax law continued throughout Gilligan's four years as Governor (1971-1975) and was necessary for the success of any bill that would benefit Ohio workers and their families. The 1970 elections produced a Democratic Governor, but a Republican-controlled General Assembly. In the 1972 elections, the Democrats captured control of the House, but still had to confront a narrow Republican majority in the Senate. Under these circumstances, the leaders of the Ohio AFL-CIO engaged in the give-and-take of political bargaining. As a result of delicate prodding, compromise, and skillful legislative maneuverings, labor recorded several significant gains for workers. Critics both in and out of the labor movement denigrated the gains as "half a loaf," but in the context of Ohio politics, in which labor more often retreated rather than advanced, "half a loaf" was much better than no loaf at all.

Ohio AFL-CIO Secretary-Treasurer Warren Smith proved particularly adept in negotiating improvements in both workers' compensation and unemployment insurance laws with the Ohio Manufacturers Association, the Ohio Chamber of Commerce, and other business groups. Since both labor and management endorsed these "negotiated bills," they sailed through the General Assembly with very little resistance. As a result, during the Gilligan years the maximum weekly workmen's compensation benefits more than doubled, climbing from $56 to $114 by mid-1974, the largest boost in the history of the fund. Moreover, labor and management, with the Legislature's concurrence, provided for an automatic annual adjustment of benefits based upon increases in the cost of living. Likewise, Smith convinced the employer associations to support an "agreed" bill that increased unemployment benefits thirty-four per cent for a claimant with four dependents and also provided for annual cost of living adjustments. For the first time, moreover, all public employees attained protection under the unemployment system. Ohio thus became the third state in the nation to have mandatory unemployment coverage for its public employees.

The Ohio AFL-CIO enjoyed another major victory with the enactment of the state's first minimum wage law. Since the merger in 1958, the organization had lobbied for a measure to protect workers not covered by federal legislation. And again, to finally attain this goal, labor had to compromise with rural interests. Thus, when the law went into effect on January 1, 1974, workers involved in intrastate commerce received $1.60 an hour, except those residing in counties with less than 300,000 residents. The law set the minimum wage in these sparsely populated counties initially at $1.40 an hour, to be raised to $1.60 in 1975. Another compromise established an agricultural minimum wage of $1.30. In exchange, the bill covered most public employees, and also provided that all employers, no matter in what county they resided, had to pay time and a half wage rates to all who worked over forty hours a week.

A host of other labor-endorsed measures cleared the General Assembly and were signed into law by Governor Gilligan. These included a strip mine reclamation bill, a consumer reform bill, and another law improving sanitation and safety conditions for migratory workers. The Ohio AFL-CIO also lobbied successfully for an act establishing the Ohio lottery to increase funding for education, and for the ratification of an amendment to the U.S. Constitution granting all citizens eighteen years of age or older the right to vote.

The Ohio AFL-CIO received sharp criticism from the middle-class oriented National Organization for Women (NOW) for its initial opposition to the Equal Rights Amendment, but labor feared the amendment would annul a host of workplace protections for women that unions had fought hard for over the years. Over the next several years, though, the Ohio AFL-CIO played a critical role in purging gender distinctions from the Ohio Code, including changing Workmen's Compensation to Workers' Compensation. Finally, reflecting an ever growing sensitivity to women's issues, the 1980 convention reversed the Ohio AFL-CIO's stance and went on record in support of the Equal Rights Amendment.

While the Ohio labor movement had always been

concerned with workplace safety and health (passing the nation's first mine safety code in the 1890s), it became intensely focused on the issue beginning in the 1970s. In 1971 alone, 419 Ohioans died in workplace accidents and another 300,000 were injured. Harry Mayfield of the Steelworkers sarcastically observed that during Rhodes' first administration the state had only seven or eight inspectors for safety and health in the workplace, yet over two hundred game wardens. Beginning in the late 1960s, however, groups like the Black Lung Association and crusaders like Ralph Nader drew public attention to dangers in the workplace, leading to the passage by the U.S. Congress in 1970 of the Occupational Safety and Health Act (OSHA).

Foremost among the labor leaders excited about the potential of the new law was Warren Smith, who was haunted by memories of his father's uncontrolled coughing brought on by fumes inhaled through long years of working in a paint shop in Lima. Shortly after becoming the Ohio AFL-CIO's Secretary-Treasurer, Smith had the organization become the guiding force in the formation of an "Ohio Breathers Lobby" which forced the permissive Rhodes administration to toughen Ohio air pollution standards. Likewise, Smith took a personal interest in implementing OSHA in Ohio. Fearing that if Ohio enacted its own safety and health standards, pro-business Republicans, would constantly maneuver to weaken them, Smith convinced Governor Gilligan to allow federal standards to prevail. He also persuaded the Governor to expand greatly the number of inspectors in the state, and helped The Ohio State University's Labor Education and Research Service receive federal grants to educate both inspectors and workers on the law's provisions.

Smith's commitment to safety and health issues — particularly those dealing with toxic substances — made the Ohio AFL-CIO the national leader in the field. In the late 1970s, he helped found the Workers' Institute for Safety and Health (WISH), attached to the Industrial Union Department of the national AFL-CIO and headquartered in Washington, D.C. The Institute's goal was to identify the health hazards and related welfare needs of workers and their families and, through research, education, and assistance, to meet those needs. From the late-1970s to the mid-1980s, Smith served as Chairman of WISH's Board of Trustees, whose membership included a number of other Ohioans including IUE President David J. Fitzmaurice, Carpenters President William Konyha, Flint Glass Workers President George Parker, United Rubber Worker President Milan Stone, Machinist President William Winpisinger, and OSU's Labor Education and Research Service Director C.J. Slanicka.

VIII

Despite the legislative gains made in the early 1970s, all was not well within the Ohio AFL-CIO nor with its relationship with the Governor. The problem centered on Frank King, who had had a distinguished political career as Democratic leader in the Ohio Senate before being recruited for the presidency of the Ohio AFL-CIO in 1964. As we have seen, the election of 1964 produced a tie between the parties in the Senate leading the Executive Board to request King to serve one more term. During these years, King played a critical role as Senate Minority Leader in fending off the anti-worker initiatives of the Rhodes administration. As head of the Ohio delegation to the 1968 Democratic National Convention, King naturally viewed himself not just as President of the Ohio AFL-CIO, but also as the leader of the state's Democratic lawmakers and as the central power within the Ohio Democratic Party. But this situation began to change when he relinquished his Senate seat in 1969 as required by a provision in the Ohio AFL-CIO Constitution which stipulated that the President and Secretary-Treasurer must be full time officers and reside in Columbus. Even out of the Senate, however, King continued to wield considerable influence through his protégé and successor as Senate Democratic leader, Anthony Calabrese. Yet that influence, too, faded upon Gilligan's election in November and his assumption of the mantle of party leadership.

King intensely disliked Gilligan, and through Calabrese and other state senators tried to assert himself as the chief policy maker for Ohio Democrats. As we have seen, throughout 1971 he opposed Gilligan's income tax proposal and led the Ohio AFL-CIO in advancing its own tax reform package. When, however, it became clear that the Legislature would not enact labor's plan, King balked at coming to an accord with Gilligan. In order to win at least "a half a loaf" in tax reform, Secretary-Treasurer Smith persuaded the Executive Board to accept the Governor's income tax initiative, much to King's displeasure. From this point on, relations between the Secretary-Treasurer and the President became strained, with Smith searching for areas to cooperate with Gilligan and King more often than not in opposition.

The feuds between King and the Governor and between King and Smith percolated over the next two years and gradually entrapped the Executive Board. During this time, Gilligan attended two meetings of the

Executive Board to reassure the members that he wanted to work closely with them. Since King was uncooperative, however, the Governor and his aides conducted most of their business with the Ohio AFL-CIO through Warren Smith, a strategy that only increased the tensions between the President and Secretary-Treasurer. On December 22, 1972, the Board spent three hours discussing the duties and responsibilities of the executive officers, concluding with a motion reaffirming support for both King and Smith. Still, the issue reappeared at the January 25, 1973, meeting of the Executive Board when the members debated whether Frank King alone or both King and Smith would be registered lobbyists for the Ohio AFL-CIO.

In March 1974, the situation reached both a critical and a comical level. At a time in history when President Richard Nixon and the Watergate break-in dominated the news, Frank King told reporters that someone working for the Governor had broken into the Ohio AFL-CIO headquarters. The actual event was less dramatic than King's hoopla, but it reveals how far relationships had deteriorated. In February 1974, King fired Public Relations Director Chuck Borsari because of his support for Smith and replaced him with William Obbagy. Borsari then went to work for the Ohio Department of Industrial Relations as an information officer. On a Friday night shortly afterwards, Warren Smith let Borsari into the state headquarters to xerox some material he had left behind. Obbagy discovered him working at the machine and notified King. President King exploded! After penning a letter to the Governor demanding an investigation of what a state employee was doing in the Federation's headquarters after hours, King held a press conference in which he fumed about the "break in."

By publicly exposing the state body's dirty linen and dragging the Governor into an internal squabble, King left the Executive Board little choice but to review his conduct. At the March 22 meeting both Harry Mayfield of the Steelworkers and Joseph Sedivy of the Building Trades charged King with being "blind with power" and not always following the policy set by the Board. A special April 26 meeting was even more of a ruckus. It took all morning and into the afternoon simply to get the minutes of the previous meeting approved. By now it was clear that King would be challenged for re-election at the Ohio AFL-CIO's upcoming May convention, so extensive maneuvering occurred over the standing of various locals favorable to one side or another.

At the April 26 meeting, Warren Smith provided the Executive Board members with a fifty-page report characterizing King as a frustrated politician, a poor administrator, and obstinately at odds with the Gilligan administration. Labeled the "Black Book" by the press, the report claimed that King controlled a block of Senate Democrats who joined with Senate Republicans to thwart programs sponsored by Governor Gilligan. In particular, it documented Frank King's failure to represent the Executive Board's position accurately on a number of issues, most notably the income tax battle. In short, Smith's report refocused the controversy away from King's disputes with the Governor or himself and onto the President's failure to carry out the official policy established by the Executive Board.

Frank King tried to defuse the issue by calling another special Executive Board meeting to discuss who conspired to compile the dastardly document, but not necessarily its substance. King contended that Chuck

Borsari was xeroxing the "Black Book" when caught in the headquarters. For an increasing number of Executive Board members, however, that issue was irrelevant and so the May 10 meeting was never convened for lack of a quorum. Various Board members and other leaders around the state now saw King as a loose cannon who needed to be replaced if the Ohio AFL-CIO was to take advantage of a supportive Governor, whom they all anticipated would be re-elected in November. To challenge King for the Federation's presidency they recruited Milan Marsh, the forty-six year old Executive Secretary of the Ohio State Council of Carpenters, who like King, could claim the loyalty of the building trades.

Tension gripped the Ninth Constitutional Convention of the Ohio AFL-CIO as it convened on May 21, 1974. While luminaries orated from the podium, pro-King and anti-King delegates scrambled around trying to round up votes. In the end, Marsh trounced King by a three-to-one margin and Smith's tally over King's running mate, Massillon Steelworker Floyd Chapman, was even greater. The election also changed the profile of the Executive Board, as several defenders of King, including six from Cleveland, went down in defeat. On the other hand the delegates made history in electing the first two women to serve on the Executive Board, Barbara Easterling of the Communications Workers of America (CWA) and Genevieve Motsinger of IUE.

IX

With Frank King's departure from the presidency, many in the Ohio AFL-CIO anticipated a golden period of cooperation between the labor movement and Governor

Gilligan, whom almost all political analysts predicted would win re-election easily in November. Most commentators viewed the Republican challenger, James Rhodes, as too old and too encumbered by the shortcomings of his first administration to be successful. Traditional sources of Republican funds wrote off the election as a Democratic victory, making it difficult for Rhodes to raise enough money to buy TV time.

Yet Rhodes had immense popular appeal, and Gilligan had an uncanny knack of alienating those from whom he needed support. In Ohio politics, Democratic candidates needed to carry Cleveland by a huge margin in order to offset Republican predominance elsewhere. Gilligan, however, took Cleveland too lightly. He failed to campaign extensively there, and the controversies surrounding King hurt Gilligan's support among some Cleveland labor leaders. James Iafelice, President of District 54 of the International Association of Machinist and Chair of the Cleveland Committee on Political Education, had backed King for re-election and consequently lost his seat on the Executive Board. Not content to let things die, he sought revenge. "I am going to give Gilligan the same thing he gave Frank King, the shaft," Iafelice declared as he publicly endorsed Rhodes.

Far more damaging than the loss of Iafelice's support was Gilligan's alienation of the Ohio Conference of Teamsters. The Conference had endorsed Gilligan on the condition that he would distance himself from the United Farm Workers (UFW), with whom the Teamsters were having a jurisdictional dispute. For whatever reason, Gilligan, nonetheless, joined UFW President Cesar Chavez at a September rally in Dayton. Learning of the betrayal, Ohio Conference of Teamsters President

Jackie Presser notified Gilligan's campaign manager that the Conference would now support Rhodes. The infusion of Teamster money into the Rhodes campaign allowed the airing of a series of television advertisements. In the closing weeks of the campaign, Rhodes gained momentum and edged ahead of Gilligan to victory.

Gilligan created his own defeat, for the rest of the labor-backed Democratic ticket did very well, capturing the other statewide offices including Lieutenant Governor and also retaining control of the General Assembly. "I blew it," Gilligan candidly confessed when reporters asked him what went wrong. No matter what the reasons were for Gilligan's loss, labor paid a steep price. Rhodes returned to the Governor's office in January 1975, determined to make Ohio friendlier to business by paring back the gains won for workers over the past four years.

Ohio trade unionists protest a 1963 attempt to undermine the State's unemployment compensation system. (Ohio AFL-CIO Collection at the Ohio Historical Society)

Ohio workers protesting proposed cuts in unemployment compensation parade in front of the Statehouse in 1963. (Ohio AFL-CIO Collection at the Ohio Historical Society)

Unionists march at an Ohio AFL-CIO-sponsored rally to defeat a bill to curtail the state's unemployment compensation system. (Ohio AFL-CIO Collection at the Ohio Historical Society)

Elmer Cope congratulates newly-elected Ohio AFL-CIO President David Kane at the 1962 Biennial Convention. (Elmer Cope Collection at the Ohio Historical Society)

Ohio AFL-CIO Secretary-Treasurer Robert Bollard (seated on the right), who succeeded Cope in the Summer of 1963, confers with delegates at the 1964 Convention. (Robert Bollard Collection at the Ohio Historical Society)

Bollard poses with newly-elected President Frank King at the 1964 Convention. (Robert Bollard Collection at the Ohio Historical Society)

The Ohio AFL-CIO helped reestablish United Organized Labor of Ohio (UOLO) in order to defeat the 1965 Republican apportionment plan. Here a UOLO speaker details the plan to a labor audience. (Ohio AFL-CIO Collection at the Ohio Historical Society)

Students at Columbus Bishop Ready High School compare union rolls with lists of registered voters as part of the Ohio AFL-CIO's *Spirit of '67* political mobilization drive. (Ohio AFL-CIO Collection at the Ohio Historical Society)

Chapter Five

Rhodes, Rust and Recession, 1975-1982

I

When James Allen Rhodes took the oath of office as Governor for a third time in January 1975, Ohio's economy differed dramatically from when he had first entered office during the boom years of the 1960s. For three decades, Ohio workers and employers had enjoyed the rewards of post-World War II prosperity and steady economic growth. From 1945 through the early 1970s, the United States had dominated world markets and enjoyed what economist John Kenneth Galbraith called the "Age of Affluence." Ohio basked fully in the prosperity, ranking among the top five states in industrial production and standing second only to Michigan in the value of its exports. The profits earned, while not equitably distributed between workers and owners, nonetheless led to the highest standard of living the world had ever seen.

By the mid-1970s, however, the "Age of Affluence" had clearly ended in Ohio. The forces undermining the golden years arose gradually and were diverse. For one, the United States' dominant position in the world market faded as other nations, most notably Germany and Japan, rebuilt their war-torn economies with the latest technology and entered into global competition. In the 1960s, American manufacturers, including many large Ohio firms, responded to this challenge by replacing workers with technology and automation, causing the number of industrial jobs to begin to decline. By the 1970s various corporations simply decided to close their aging facilities in the Buckeye State and build modern plants elsewhere. Seeking lax labor standards, low taxes, and minimal government regulation, these firms either migrated from the "Rustbelt" to the "Sunbelt" or set up shop in "developing" third-world nations.

To compound the problems arising from the restructuring of the industrial world, an "energy crisis" plagued Ohio throughout the 1970s and further depressed the state's economy. Beginning with the Arab oil embargo of 1973, the crisis deepened in 1975 when American natural gas companies curtailed production to force deregulation of the industry. The oil crisis crippled America's automobile and related industries, sending them into their worst financial period since the Great Depression, while the natural gas crisis forced numerous factories in the state to shut down for lack of fuel. The extremely harsh winter of 1976-77, followed by the blizzard of 1978, only made a bad situation worse by further depleting energy supplies and forcing schools, factories, and public agencies to close.

Ohioans did not fare well in the emerging "post-industrial" world. For a century, the state's economy had relied heavily on manufacturing, which employed just over half of all nonagricultural workers by the end of World War II. Yet, by 1980 economic changes reduced that percentage to only twenty-nine. Between 1969 and 1977,

Ohio's eight most industrialized counties lost an average of sixteen percent of their manufacturing jobs. In the Dayton area, manufacturing jobs fell by twenty-five percent, while Cuyahoga County suffered an eighteen percent lost. The situation became even bleaker in the early 1980s. The Ohio Bureau of Employment Services calculated that the state lost 162,000 manufacturing jobs between 1980 and 1982 alone, the biggest drop in the nation. Akron abdicated its title as the "tire capital of the world" as Firestone, Goodyear, and Goodrich ceased manufacturing operations there idling 8,000 workers. Yet it was the Youngstown-Warren area that became the symbol of the social cost of industrial relocation when Youngstown Sheet and Tube and U.S. Steel closed their mills. With over 10,000 workers laid off, the area's unemployment rate stood at fifteen percent, the highest since the bleak 1930s.

Some of Ohio's dislocated workers found new employment in the growing service sector of the economy. "By 1970," according to historians Raymond Boryczka and Lorin Lee Cary, "fifty-four percent of the employed workforce generated services and by 1980 nearly sixty-seven percent did." Between 1980 and 1982 the state gained 30,000 jobs in the health care field alone. Yet, this shift to service employment actually eroded Ohio workers' purchasing power. In the late 1970s, non-manufacturing workers only took home about $200 weekly, while the diminishing number of factory workers earned better than $300 per week. "The combination of declining purchasing power and rising unemployment," Boryczka and Cary observed, "had a deadly effect within the state — eating away at the tax base and accumulated manufacturing skills while accelerating the decline of major urban centers."

II

Just as the transition to a "post-industrial" society disrupted the lives of Ohio workers, it also severely impacted on the state's labor movement. As the manufacturing workforce declined and plants closed, the size and strength of the state's largest unions diminished. Between 1970 and 1978, Ohio union membership fell by over nine percent, the sharpest drop among the major industrial states. Still, the picture of the ebb and flow of union membership is complex. As industrial unions like the Rubber Workers and IUE waned in numbers, new unions in the service and public sectors grew. Although such gains failed to offset the membership losses among the manufacturing-based unions, still by the 1980s the American Federation of State, County, and Municipal Employees (AFSCME), the American Federation of Teachers (AFT), the Communications Workers, and the Service Employees (SEIU) spoke with an increasingly louder voice in Ohio's labor circles.

The hard times, plant closings, and declining union membership also adversely affected the Ohio AFL-CIO. Income to the state headquarters stagnated as local unions paid per capita taxes on fewer members and a significant number of locals sought to cut expenses by disaffiliating. Between the 1978 and 1980 conventions, for instance, the state body lost over 7,000 members. The Ohio AFL-CIO's forty-six percent affiliation rate by local unions in 1980 ranked well below the national average of fifty-two percent.

Yet, the state body's financial crisis was more complicated than simply a decline in membership equating to a decline in per capita tax income. In the 1970s a new term, "stagflation," entered the American vocabulary as the nation faced the simultaneous existence of recession and inflation. Within the depressed Ohio economy, expenses for the Federation continued to rise. Double-digit inflation quickly gobbled up the per capita increase in dues approved in 1970. *Focus* proved especially expensive as both printing and mailing costs soared. Whereas in 1968, $833 mailed the first *Focus* to 800,000 unionists, it took $18,000 to reach the same readership a decade later. To pare back expenditures, the state body published only five issues of the monthly magazine in 1976 instead of the initial goal of nine. As publishing and postage costs continued to rise, the federation decided in 1981 to produce only four issues annually and to rename the magazine *Focus Quarterly*.

Political action expenses also rose dramatically during the 1970s and 1980s. Throughout the 1960s, the Ohio AFL-CIO had squirreled away funds during the odd number years to pay for the political campaigns during the even numbered election years. Stagflation ended this strategy, and in 1975 the state body ran a small deficit. With up to a third of the state's 850,000 unionists changing addresses between elections, the cost of updating the much-acclaimed computerized databank amounted to $110,000 for the 1976 election alone. In addition, TV advertisements, mailings, political rallies, telephone banks, and a host of other activities drove the cost of political activities far beyond income.

Secretary-Treasurer Warren Smith proved a master at maneuvering, borrowing, and begging the needed funds. He also forthrightly educated Executive Board members and convention delegates on the need to increase per capita taxes. Thus, under his guidance, both the 1976 and 1980 conventions raised dues. The new revenues, when offset by the effects of stagflation, kept the organization solvent but not affluent. Moreover, Smith, while clearly not a spendthrift, committed every dollar available to address labor's immediate needs rather than accumulating extensive reserves.

Despite tight funds and shrinking personnel, the Federation continued to expand and enrich its services and programs for affiliates. Disregarding the financial pinch, the Ohio AFL-CIO spent more on communicating with the rank-and-file than any other state AFL-CIO. John R. Thomas, who became the organization's Public Relations Director in 1977, redesigned *Focus* and *News & Views*, but maintained their exceptional quality. In 1981, *Focus Quarterly* earned an "Award of Honor" from the International Labor Press Association for overall excellence and an "Award of Merit" for use of graphics and photographs. Starting in 1978, the Ohio AFL-CIO produced a monthly radio news program which provided free labor-oriented programming to more than seventy stations around the state. In 1981 the International Labor Press Association recognized this pioneering effort with an "Award of Merit," and singled out the radio show's Labor Day coverage for an "Award of Honor."

The state body conducted various other activities on a pay-as-you-go basis. Under Tom Bell, who also joined the staff in 1977, the Compensation Department ran a high quality Workers' Compensation Institute that affiliates judged well worth the price of admission. They also recognized the importance of annual editions of the *Workers' Compensation Manual*, the *Occupational Disease Manual*, and *Workers' Compensation Facts*, far-and-away the best publications of their kind in the nation. Other programming sponsored by the state body, including the always well-attended annual conferences on civil rights issues, also met expenses through registration fees.

In many instances, however, the state body turned to The Ohio State University's Labor Education and Research Service (LERS), led by Professor C.J. Slanicka, to fulfill programming needs. Funded by a labor-backed line item in the state budget, LERS co-sponsored programs with the Federation, central bodies, and individual locals on an array of subjects from stewards training to labor law. Under the Ohio AFL-CIO's guidance, LERS conducted the annual summer school at Kenyon College. It also organized the Ohio AFL-CIO's first Women's Conference in 1975, as well as the Safety and Health Institutes beginning in 1979. In 1976 it produced the documentary film "Strength through Struggle," which won first prize in a film competition sponsored by the International Labor Press Association as well as other honors. By 1980, LERS annually conducted over 275 educational programs involving almost 10,000 union members from around the state. Clearly, LERS's close working relationship with the state body enabled the Ohio AFL-CIO to sponsor activities far beyond what it otherwise could have done during these lean years.

III

All the while Ohio languished in economic malaise, it also suffered from divided political leadership. For most of these years Democrats prevailed in the General Assembly, while Republican Governor James Rhodes reigned over the state's vast administrative bureaucracy. Sixty-six years old in 1975, Rhodes' agenda for the state was more suited for the earlier era of post-war affluence. As during his first two terms, Rhodes pushed policies favoring business at the expense of education and social services.

The Governor's panacea for Ohio's economic woes — his "Blueprint for Ohio" — called for massive, long-term tax-abatements for new and expanding businesses and four bond issues to underwrite urban renewal, housing development, transportation, and public construction. The colossal bond program, which Rhodes announced during his January 1975 inaugural address, constituted the largest package of debt in Ohio history. Shortly after taking office, Rhodes met with the Ohio AFL-CIO Executive Board to discuss his proposals. Although he claimed that the bond issues were necessary "to produce jobs," the Executive Board concluded that Rhodes' proposals would not live up to the Governor's boasts, which grew more expansive every time he gave a speech. Rather, the Board saw the program as too costly for any temporary benefit that might be gained. Consequently, the Ohio AFL-CIO joined several other organizations, including the League of Women Voters and the Council of Churches, in a coalition to defeat all the issues except the one to promote low-income housing.

When the votes were counted in November 1975, widespread public resentment against the Governor's tax giveaways to business, his "Christmas Tree" pork barrel for favored politicians, and his extravagant highway building plans led to the rejection of the entire package. With four out of five voters saying "no" to the bond issues, Rhodes suffered one of the most convincing defeats in Ohio history. "The people made up their minds that this was a boondoggle," Warren Smith told reporters. "Once they saw they were misled, they totally rejected what they saw as the grand swindle of the century." The defeat stung Rhodes, who for the next seven years shied away from advancing any program that would significantly reshape Ohio's economic future.

Yet if the Governor lacked a grand vision of how to lead the state into its post-industrial future, he nonetheless knew how to keep his political opponents at bay. From his earlier stint as Governor, Rhodes knew how to use his executive powers to block Democratic legislative initiatives. Under his watchful eye, for instance, a series of laws passed during Gilligan's last week in office simply went uncertified by the Republican Lieutenant Governor John Brown, a move which allowed Republican Secretary of State Ted Brown to declare them not formally passed. Once in office, Rhodes freely used his veto power to nullify reforms of workers' compensation, unemployment insurance, voter reforms, public employee collective bargaining, and a host of other measures coming out of the Legislature. In 1976 alone, he turned back over two dozen bills. And if the General Assembly overroad a veto, he found ways to limit the law's impact. Rhodes, for example, reduced funds for consumer protection, a move that basically made enforcement ineffective, claiming the need to retrench in order to balance the budget.

In order to honor a campaign pledge to the business community, Rhodes particularly sought to trim the state's much-acclaimed occupational safety and health program. Under the Governor's watchful eye, Helen Evans, the Director of the Department of Industrial Relations, and her assistant Sam McAdow, worked with

President Gerald Ford's OSHA appointees to end federal funding of the state's inspection program. In early January 1976, the Ohio AFL-CIO obtained and made public copies of correspondence detailing the negotiations. Exposure of the plan prompted Speaker of the House Vernal G. Riffe to call for a full-scale inquiry, causing Rhodes to do a political-shuffle and keep the safety inspector program running a while longer.

Not accepting setbacks graciously, in January 1976, Rhodes sought to gain control of the Bureau of Workers' Compensation by firing Gregory Stebbins as the Chairman of the Ohio Industrial Commission. A former Compensation Director for the Ohio AFL-CIO and International Representative for the United Steelworkers, Stebbins had been appointed to the post by Gilligan and was the sole Democrat on the Commission. Rhodes accused the Commissioner of using his post for personal gain and engaging in conflicts of interest, even though a Franklin County Grand Jury found that Stebbins had done no wrong. After a U.S. District Court Judge ordered Stebbins reinstated at the Industrial Commission, Rhodes asked the Ohio Senate to rescind its 1972 confirmation of Stebbins. Through pressure from the Ohio AFL-CIO, Stebbins retained his seat until his term expired in August 1977. After that, Rhodes exercised unobstructed control over the Commission and its subordinate Bureau of Workers' Compensation.

Such cat-and-mouse maneuvers between the Governor and the Ohio AFL-CIO continued through Rhodes' years in office. Yet, as political realists both labor and Rhodes searched for issues, however small, on which they could cooperate. Rhodes loved a political fight and felt that he had worthy opponents among the state's labor leaders. In one very dramatic episode, he appeared uninvited and alone at a retirement dinner for UAW leader Ray Ross to give his own personal testimonial to a man with whom he seldom agreed but deeply respected. Still, despite such personable gestures, in the final analysis Ohio's longest serving Governor resisted far more often than he advanced the reforms advocated by labor.

IV

Despite obstructions from Governor Rhodes, the Ohio AFL-CIO made considerable progress on its legislative agenda between 1975 and 1978. The 1974 elections gave the Democrats control of the General Assembly for the first time in over a decade. With Vern Riffe as Speaker of the House and Oliver Ocasek as the Majority Leader of the Senate, the General Assembly enacted improvements in workers' compensation, unemployment insurance, and the state's minimum wage. Prodded by labor, the Legislature also required supermarkets to provide visual prices on items even if they used bar codes, utilities to use a more consumer-oriented formula when determining rates, and gas companies to stop charging homeowners for natural gas purchased expressly for business uses. Warren Pate, the Ohio AFL-CIO Civil Rights Director, played a critical role in convincing the General Assembly to designate the third Monday of January an official state holiday celebrating the legacy of Dr. Martin Luther King, Jr. "It is difficult to recall a better Legislature than the 111th," Milan Marsh and Warren Smith informed delegates to the 1976 convention. "From the first day of the opening gavel . . . until its recent recess, the working people of Ohio finally got an even break."

Still, Governor Rhodes vetoed many major pieces of labor-endorsed legislation, including one granting public employees collective bargaining rights and another reforming the voter registration system. Thus, the Ohio AFL-CIO entered the 1976 political season determined to elect a "veto proof" General Assembly. Borrowing heavily to finance the campaign, the state body fine-tuned its political action program as never before. In the two months prior to the November election it mailed out fifty-seven different regional editions of *Focus* to publicize its endorsement of specific candidates in given localities.

Labor provided the muscle in the Democratic Party's effort, and the results were rewarding. Sixty-six percent of the candidates for the Ohio House endorsed by the Ohio AFL-CIO's Committee on Political Education (COPE) won, and ten out of fifteen endorsees won in Senate races. An elated Warren Smith felt that "the 1976 COPE effort was the most substantial and most successful COPE program ever conducted by the Ohio AFL-CIO." Vice President William Sheehan readily agreed, noting that it was the best operation he had ever witnessed. Not only did the Democrats strengthen their control over the General Assembly, but Howard Metzenbaum bested Robert Taft to join John Glenn in the United States Senate. With increasing focus on judicial elections, the Ohio AFL-CIO helped William Sweeney and Ralph S. Locher win seats on the state's Supreme Court, as Democrats took control of that body for the first time since 1960. Important as these victories proved to be, most post-election analysts concentrated on the key role labor played in delivering Ohio, and therefore the presidency, to Jimmy Carter.

Having elected enough Democrats to the General Assembly to override any veto by the Governor, the Ohio AFL-CIO expected to make dramatic gains. And to some degree it did. The Democratic-dominated Legislature established a Worker Rehabilitation Program that gave injured workers the opportunity to return to their old jobs or find employment commensurate with their skills. Thus, Ohio became the first state in the nation to offer complete rehabilitation as an alternative to forcing totally disabled workers to spend the rest of their lives on Workers' Compensation. In the area of consumer affairs, the Legislature passed a partial "lifeline" law that helped senior citizens and the handicapped with their winter heating bills. It also enacted a bill that allowed pharmacists to substitute equally effective generic drugs for brand name prescription medicine.

The most dramatic success for the Ohio AFL-CIO came when the Democratic-controlled General Assembly reformed the state's voter registration procedures over solid Republican opposition and a veto by Governor Rhodes. The bill, which gave Ohio the nation's most progressive registration and voting laws, permitted door-to-door and workplace registration drives, and it allowed people to sign-up to vote when they registered their car or obtained a driver's license. Most controversial, the law provided for Election Day registration and for permanent registration.

Unable to block the law's passage, the Republicans and their business allies sought to weaken the Voter Reform Act. First, they relied on Secretary of State Ted Brown to delay carrying out its provisions, only to have the new Democratic-dominated Supreme Court order him to implement it immediately. The opponents then placed on the November 1977 ballot a constitutional amendment to forbid Election Day and permanent registration. With the UAW, League of Women Voters, Urban League, NAACP, and Council of Churches, the Ohio AFL-CIO immediately established the Citizens' Committee to Fight Issue 1. Despite a mammoth effort, however, the proponents of Issue 1 carried the day by outspending the Citizens' Committee and saturating TV in the closing days of the campaign. Accepting the set-back graciously, Ohio AFL-CIO President Milan Marsh reminded the Executive Board that the rest of the provisions contained in the Voter Reform Act remained law, giving Ohio "the best registration law outside of those states which have election day registration."

Out of the unsuccessful campaign to defeat Issue 1 emerged the first signs of labor's growing frustration with the state's Democratic Party. During a post-election analysis at the January 25, 1978, Executive Board Meeting, President Milan Marsh commented bitterly that "those who were leading the fight against Issue #1 had difficulty with the Democratic Party, which wasn't willing to come out and fight vigorously."

This anger grew more intense in 1978 as the Democrats proved shaky allies in labor's quest for a public employee collective bargaining law. As it had in 1975, in 1977 the Democratic-controlled General Assembly passed such a bill. And as he had in 1975, Governor Rhodes again vetoed it. However, this time the Ohio AFL-CIO expected to win because it had worked hard to rejuvenate the Ohio Democratic Party and to elect a "veto proof" Legislature. Nonetheless, although the Senate overrode the Governor's veto along straight party lines, the House Democrats divided and failed to carry the day. Two Democratic Representatives, William Hinig of New Philadelphia and Arthur Bowers of Steubenville, refused to override the veto, and Speaker Riffe failed to apply his legendary pressure to keep them in line.

Tempers flared when the Ohio AFL-CIO Executive Board members met on March 31 to discuss the defeat of the public employees collective bargaining bill. With Vice President Ed Fire insisting that the organization raise "hell" with the Democrats, President Milan Marsh recounted a recent meeting with party officials in which he expressed "disapproval with the Democratic party in failing as a party to support labor legislation." Marsh then suggested that "perhaps the best way to get the party's attention is by giving them a 'whack' in the pocketbook."

Rather than take such drastic action, the Board elected to withdraw all support from Bowers and to join AFSCME and the Ohio Education Association in a campaign against Hinig in the upcoming May primary. This strategy, though, led to further tension with the Democrats as Speaker of the House Vern Riffe sent staff and money to help Hinig. "In affect," Warren Smith told Board Members, "we are fighting our own money since the Ohio AFL-CIO contributed large sums of money to the Democratic leadership in the House for campaign purposes. Despite Hinig's breaking with a major Democratic policy position, the House leadership has made this a fight between Labor and the Democrats rather than a matter of Democratic policy."

By August the situation between labor and the Democrats had deteriorated to the point that Warren Smith felt that "the organization hadn't had a worse year in the Legislature since 1967 when the Republicans were in complete control." Citing unsuccessful bills on pricing, lie detectors, workers' compensation, unemployment insurance, public employee collective bargaining, and graduated municipal income taxes, Smith told Executive Board members that the General Assembly's record was so bad that it was impossible to put together a voting record. Vice President Harry Mayfield observed that "legislative leaders were trying to teach the organization a lesson over the effort to defeat State Representative William Hinig in the primary election." Milan Marsh concluded that the only way to improve labor's fate with the party was to elect Dick Celeste as Governor in November, which would realign leadership among the Democrats.

Following Marsh's advice, the Ohio AFL-CIO's big push in the election of 1978 centered on statewide races. *Focus* sent out only twenty-five special editions to boost state legislators and other local candidates, as compared to fifty-seven two years before. Yet those supported by labor did very well, as seventy-five per cent of labor-backed candidates seeking statewide office won. Among those elected were Frank D. Celebrezze as Chief Justice of the Ohio Supreme Court and William D. Brown, re-elected as an Associate Justice. The judicial victories guaranteed continued Democratic control of the high court. Another major victory came when Tony Celebrezze ousted twenty-eight-year Secretary of State Ted Brown by only 8,000 votes. In Congressional and General Assembly races, the winning rate for COPE-endorsed candidates approached sixty percent. Still, in the face of a general labor/Democratic victory, James Rhodes' popularity held, as he defeated Richard Celeste in a contest notable for its extremely low voter turnout.

The November 1978 elections did not improve labor's standing with Democratic legislators. In their *Officers' Report* to the 1980 Convention, Milan Marsh and Warren Smith roasted the 113th General Assembly as "one of the most disappointing in many years of control by majority Democrats. With few exceptions, the Legislature has turned a deaf ear to the needs of working people while extending a welcoming hand to corporate interests in Ohio." Relationships deteriorated so badly by early 1979 that the Ohio AFL-CIO Executive Board passed a resolution distancing itself from the state Democratic party through a policy of non-participation in dinners and other affairs. Not surprisingly then, the organizations greatest victory in 1979 came outside the legislative chambers. Fearing that a ban against throw away cans and bottles would cost the state 10,000 jobs and $80,000,000 in wages, the Ohio AFL-CIO joined business and industry groups to defeat mandatory deposit legislation.

Labor's political fortunes finally hit the lowest point in a decade with the election of 1980. Although still frustrated over the Democratic Party's lackluster commitment to labor's legislative goals, the Ohio AFL-CIO Committee on Political Education vigorously endorsed and funded that party's candidates. Yet the winds of conservatism sweeping the nation left their chill on Ohio. Ronald Reagan won the presidency by a landslide, the Federation's Ohio Fair Tax Initiative went down to defeat, Republicans re-captured control of the Ohio Senate, and the Democratic hold on the House shrank to a handful of votes. With a Republican Governor and Senate, and what Warren Smith politely characterized as "lack of positive leadership in the House," the Ohio AFL-CIO spent the 115th session of the

Ohio General Assembly on the defense. Clearly, the time had arrived for a new strategy to re-coop labor's political influence.

V

While the leaders of the Ohio AFL-CIO bemoaned the performance of the Democrats they helped elect to the General Assembly, they were delighted with the candidates they supported for the Ohio Supreme Court. For years the Ohio AFL-CIO's Committee on Political Education had endorsed individuals for the high bench, but had not participated in their campaigns with the same intensity it had in other statewide races. This policy changed in 1976 when the organization increased its publicity and funding for William Sweeney and Ralph S. Locher. Their victory gave the Democrats a four to three margin on the Court and control of the bench for the first time since 1960. Seeing how beneficial a favorable judiciary could be, in 1978 the Ohio AFL-CIO went all out to elect Frank D. Celebrezze as Chief Justice and re-elect William B. Brown to the Supreme Court.

Increased involvement in Supreme Court races meant not only financing a large portion of the races, but also teaching the candidates how to campaign. Traditionally, candidates for the high bench stood for office without campaigning, and as a result most voters paid little attention to who was on the ballot. Now, under Warren Smith's tutorage, candidates learned how to dress and greet people in a manner that generated a positive reaction and to produce TV spots that made their names known. In intensifying the campaigns for the Supreme

Court, the Ohio AFL-CIO lead the Democratic Party, and also got the jump on the Republicans.

The newly configured Court issued decisions favorable to labor on a range of subjects from apportionment to prevailing wage. Yet the most notable change in the Court's position concerned workers' compensation. On June 25, 1980, for instance, the Ohio Supreme Court issued a landmark decision overturning a Court of Appeal's ruling in *Green vs. International Harvester*. In the *Green* case, the high court ended the employer's practice of offsetting workers' compensation awards by the amount paid under pension disability plans. As a result, thousands of injured Ohio workers received millions of dollars in additional compensation.

Two years later, the Ohio Supreme Court made another critical decision in the case of *Blakenship vs. Cincinnati Milicron*. Written by Chief Justice Frank Celebrezze (whom *Forbes* magazine labeled "the hanging judge of business"), the decision permitted workers to sue their employer if the latter introduced health hazards into the workplace without telling the workers. In other words, employers could no longer take refuge behind the workers' compensation system (which, for the most part, protects them against negligence) if they commit intentional torts or wrongs against workers.

In August 1982, the Supreme Court approved the use of interest earned on the workers' compensation fund to provide payment to permanently and totally disabled workers who qualify for the Disabled Worker Relief Fund program. In overturning a ruling by the Franklin County Court of Appeals, the Court preserved the income of 14,000 people dependent upon the fund. Decisions such as these led Warren Smith to tell the Executive Board in

March 1982, that "the work and money involved in State Supreme Court races are beginning to pay off for injured workers."

VI

Following the electoral setback in November 1980, the Ohio AFL-CIO quickly regained the offensive, helped in part by the brashness of anti-worker, anti-union forces. Nationally, the Reagan administration made clear its desire to weaken social programs and gut the Occupational Safety and Health Administration. In August 1981, Reagan sent a message to labor by smashing the Professional Air Traffic Controllers Organization (PATCO). At the state level, Governor Rhodes, the Republican majority in the Senate, and business interests sought to freeze unemployment insurance benefits. They also worked to limit the right of injured workers and consumers to sue manufacturers for faulty products and proposed solving the state's financial crisis by increasing the tax burden on consumers. Clearly, Ohio's working people faced the worst economic conditions and the most unsympathetic government since the Great Depression of the 1930s.

Significant as these factors were, it is important to emphasize that the Ohio AFL-CIO had laid the foundation over the previous two decades for is electoral successes in 1981 and 1982. Prior to 1960, rural, usually Republican, conservatives controlled the state government because their counties were over-represented in the Legislature and election laws made it difficult for blue-collar workers to vote. To overcome these hurdles, the Ohio AFL-CIO successfully fought for more just apportionment in the 1960s and pushed for major reforms which made it easier for people to register and vote in the

1970s. These accomplishments, along with *The Spirit of '67*, greatly improved the chances of labor-backed candidates. By the early 1980s, labor leaders could confidently assert that "success can usually be guaranteed since a cohesive Labor vote is sufficiently large enough to make the difference between victory and defeat in any race."

Ironically, the first step in labor's political ascendancy came with the help of some very unlikely allies. At the very time that the Ohio AFL-CIO was sparring with the Ohio Manufacturers Association and the Ohio Chamber of Commerce over the appropriate steps to rebuild the solvency of the state's unemployment insurance fund, the three organizations, along with others, joined ranks to defend Ohio's workers' compensation program.

In 1981 out-of-state insurance companies and the Independent Insurance Agents Association of Ohio formed a front organization called the Ohio Committee for Free Enterprise Competition. Spending thousands of dollars to collect signatures, the Committee placed upon the November ballot Issue 1 to allow private companies to sell workers' compensation insurance, thus undermining the state's highly praised exclusively state-run program. In the early 1980s, however, neither labor nor management desired to privatize the system since employers enjoyed the nation's 39th lowest workers' compensation premiums and workers received the 6th highest level of benefits. Convinced that the passage of Issue 1 would allow private insurers to skim off the low-risk businesses, the Ohio AFL-CIO and business associations feared that only high risk firms would be left in the state run system thus forcing increased premiums and lower benefits. While the insurance industry significantly outspent the coalition against the proposal, labor's unprecedented mobilization of the rank-and-file led to Issue 1's defeat by a four to one margin. In Cuyahoga County alone, the number of union members voting ran ahead of the general population by around 35 percent. And on the coattails of this victory, labor also defeated Issue 2 that would have changed the method of apportioning the state in a fashion that opened the door to greater gerrymandering.

Although quickly abandoned by its business allies, the Ohio AFL-CIO sustained the momentum developed in fighting Issue 1 into the November 1982 gubernatorial elections. Throughout the year the Ohio AFL-CIO continued working closely with the central bodies on voter registration efforts. These drives paid unusually high dividends as the reform laws passed in the 1970s made it possible for volunteer deputy registrars to sign-up workers right at the job-site. As the election approached, sixty regional editions of *Focus Quarterly* were published to communicate the organization's stance on Ohio House and Senate candidates, as compared to only twenty-five special editions for the 1980 election.

Under the battle cry of "Let's Turn it Around," workers marched to the polls on election day in such numbers as to set a new record for voter participation in a non-presidential election. And their votes made a difference. For the first time since 1936, the entire labor-backed, statewide team swept the field. With Richard Celeste heading the ticket, the Democrats enjoyed a rare landslide. For the first time in decades, labor's friends controlled the Governor's office, both houses of the General Assembly, the Ohio Supreme Court, both U.S.

Senator seats, and the offices of Secretary of State, Attorney General, Auditor, and Treasurer. Rightly, Ohio's labor leadership looked toward the future with great optimism.

Chapter Six

"Our History is One of Peaks and Gullies," 1983-1993

I

On the morning of January 10, 1983, Richard F. "Dick" Celeste took the oath of office as Ohio's sixty-fourth Governor. Not since the Great Depression of the 1930s had an incoming chief executive faced such dismal conditions. After losing 246,553 manufacturing jobs between 1972 and 1982, Ohio's unemployment rate stood at fourteen percent on inaugural day. Strapped for both funds and ideas, government under the departing administration had approached a standstill. In his last years in office, observed historian George Knepper, Rhodes "gave the impression of merely holding on . . . . The governor appeared to have lost heart: he refused to push for the long-term policies and revenue sources which would help Ohio meet its critical needs."

In contrast to the graying Rhodes, the forty-five year-old Celeste exuded the energy and vigor of his ideal, John F. Kennedy. On that cold and drizzly inaugural morning, Celeste announced his "action agenda." "Stand with me," he summoned Ohioans, "because together we can begin to put our people back to work." Wanting to make government an "agent for changing," the new Governor sought to better the lives of everyone, but particularly those with special needs — youth, minorities, handicapped, mentally ill, elderly, and unemployed.

Two hours after delivering his inaugural address, Governor Celeste and his wife Dagmar appeared at 271 East State Street and interrupted an Ohio AFL-CIO Executive Board meeting. Celeste earnestly thanked the Board for labor's support in the past election and chatted briefly about plans for the next four years. The incoming Governor knew well that the Ohio AFL-CIO, engineered by Warren Smith, had played a critical role in the Democrats' victory. Not only had Celeste won the Governor's office, the Democrats controlled the General Assembly and other key state offices. Not since 1959 had the Democrats held such a commanding position.

Even before the Celestes' visit, discussion at the January 10 Executive Board meeting centered on how to take full advantage of the political situation. The more experienced members were well aware that such opportunities in history were fleeting. Consequently, Secretary-Treasurer Warren Smith placed the long-sought goals of public employee collective bargaining and toxic labeling at the top of labor's agenda. President Milan Marsh emphasized the need to ensure that both state and municipal governments enforce the prevailing wage laws on all government-funded projects. In particular, he insisted that prevailing wages be paid on multi-unit housing funded under the recent voter-approved, state-backed, low-interest mortgage loan program.

Toward the end of the meeting, Board Members granted Warren Smith a leave of absence so he could assume the directorship of the Ohio Department of

Transportation. Hoping to give his administration "a more representative appearance," Celeste named numerous women, African-Americans, and union representatives to high level positions. Despite Smith's reluctance, the Executive Board felt it was in labor's interest to have a union leader in the Governor's cabinet so as to balance the business executives whom Celeste also courted. Since Smith had every intention of returning to the Ohio AFL-CIO, the Board decided to leave his position vacant. In the interlude, the staff was to pick up the Secretary-Treasurer's duties, with Smith providing informal advice.

Smith was one of several people from the labor community placed in influential positions by the Celeste administration. Whereas Rhodes had used his gubernatorial powers to thwart labor, Celeste proved generally cooperative. To be sure, Celeste and labor disagreed on some key issues, such as when the Governor signed Senate Bill 307, a pro-business revision of the workers' compensation system, over labor's protest. However, in the broader view, throughout the 1980s Celeste and the Democratic majority in the Ohio House stood in labor's corner far more often than not.

II

The Ohio AFL-CIO took immediate advantage of the Democratic Party's dominance by pursuing a public employee collective bargaining bill. By 1980 almost all of the states in the nation permitted public employees to organize and bargain collectively, and a good number had highly detailed laws to guide such activities. Ohio, however, remained outside the fold. Rather, the Ferguson Act, passed during the anti-union hysteria of 1947, undermined free collective bargaining by making it illegal for Ohio public employees to strike. The law served more to hinder amiable resolutions of differences than it did to stem worker militancy. During the bleak 1970s, the combination of declining tax bases, layoffs, and inflation led firemen, police, prison guards, teachers, refuse collectors, social workers, hospital employees, and other public employees throughout Ohio to hit the picket line in defiance of the law. Twice during the Rhodes administration, bills to repeal the Ferguson Act and establish a system of public employee collective bargaining cleared the General Assembly only to be vetoed by the Governor. The Democratic landslide in the 1982 election assured that a new bill would not suffer the same fate.

Throughout the Winter of 1983, leaders from the Ohio AFL-CIO, AFSCME, Ohio Civil Service Employees Association (OCSEA), and other public worker unions finalized their strategy to attain collective bargaining rights. In March, state Senator Eugene Branstool of Utica, whom the Ohio AFL-CIO had struggled hard to elect, introduce Senate Bill 133. Not only did the measure repeal the Ferguson Act and allow non-safety forces to strike as a last resort, it also established a timetable for negotiating disputes and created a State Employment Relations Board (SERB) to administer the law. Strong opposition to the measure came from county and local governments, a number of the state's major newspapers and TV stations, the usual anti-union coalitions of business and civic groups, and the Republican Party. Nonetheless, Speaker of the House Vern Riffe led a comfortable majority of Democratic Representatives for easy passage in the lower chamber. In the Senate, however, the measure passed along straight party lines by only one vote. On July 6, Governor Celeste signed the law, which went into effect on April 1, 1984. At last Ohio's 600,000 public sector employees, about twelve percent of the state's workforce, could exercise the collective bargaining rights that workers in the private sector had enjoyed since the passage of the National Labor Relations Act in 1935.

After the passage of the collective bargaining bill, the Ohio AFL-CIO turned to helping the Governor secure a desperately needed increase in state revenues. The loss of industry and the recessions of the 1970s and early 1980s had left the state treasury in dire straits. With the state facing a huge deficit, public service after public service deteriorated as the Buckeye State fell further behind in national comparisons. Lack of income, for instance, led Ohio to rank among the worst in mental health care, with several state-run facilities unable to meet certification standards. Likewise, the state's education system, already poorly funded, sank deeper into distress. During the 1970s, the Governor and General Assembly continually cut state support for primary and secondary education to deal with budget problems. At one point, as more and more schools struggled to find the money needed to stay open, the only solution that Rhodes and the Legislature could conjure was a bill simply prohibiting them from closing. In 1982, Rhodes finally submitted to the inevitable and led the General Assembly in passing an increase in personal income tax. By cunningly making his tax increase "temporary," due to expire six months after he left office, Rhodes both continued to claim that he never permanently raised taxes and dumped the burden of solving the state's financial woes on his successor.

Celeste, like Gilligan and DiSalle before him, accepted the political risks of a tax increase and did what needed to be done. In his first budget, Celeste not only proposed making Rhodes' "temporary" tax hike permanent, but also added a further increase of his own. The Ohio AFL-CIO was not thrilled about endorsing the Governor's plan, but it saw no viable alternative to keep the state solvent. So too did the more astute businessmen in the state, who agreed that Ohio's parsimony had gotten out of hand. Still, from Republican politicos and conservative ideologues came wails of extravagance and profligacy. As with the public employee collective bargaining bill, Celeste's tax proposal needed the votes of all sixteen Democratic Senators to pass over the fifteen vote Republican minority. In one of the most dramatic moments in Ohio politics, Senator Oliver Ocasek rushed from Florida, where his wife was hospitalized in serious condition after an auto accident. "A hush fell over the proceedings," *Dayton Daily News* Statehouse Bureau Chief Tim Miller wrote, "as a stoop-shoulder Ocasek whispered his 'yes' and the tax package passed by one vote."

Yet, the tax battle was not over. Right-wing opponents, dreaming of a "tax rebellion" like one recently experienced in California, secured enough signatures to place two issues on the November 1983 ballot. "Issue 3" sought to overturn the recently enacted tax package as well as all other revenue measures passed since January 1, 1983. "Issue 2" would go a step further and make it more difficult to enact tax increases in the future by requiring a sixty percent affirmative vote in both houses of the Ohio Legislature instead of a simple majority. While moderate-Republicans remained mute, organized labor joined various progressive groups in challenging the tax repeal proposal that, no matter how popular it appeared, would thrust the state into chaos and probably result in even higher taxes on consumers sometime in the future.

During the campaign, the Ohio AFL-CIO emphasized that passage of Issue 2 violated majority rule. By requiring a 3/5th majority to pass a revenue-raising bill, Issue 2 would lead to vote-trading and special interest pressures, reducing the Ohio Legislature to "an auction house where the highest bid would be sought." Issue 3, labor contended, was equally unwise since it would not only terminate Celeste's tax increase but would nullify an arrangement mutually agreed upon by management and labor to raise the unemployment system out of a deficit and onto stable footing. As in the general elections, Celeste counted on labor to get out the votes and he was not disappointed as both proposals suffered defeat.

Celeste's tax increase came at an opportune moment as the economic recovery already enjoyed by most of the nation began to affect Ohio. Wall Street responded to the tax increase by raising the state's bond ratings and lowering the interest Ohio had to pay on its debts. With a slow but steady rise in employment through the mid- and late-1980s, the new tax brought in more revenue than anticipated. As a consequence, the Celeste administration repaired much of the state's infrastructure by providing increased funding for elementary and secondary education, higher education, welfare, mental health, and other state services.

In 1983 and early 1984 cautious journalists and conservative Republicans publicly criticized Celeste, the Democratic-controlled General Assembly, and the labor movement for pushing their political program too fast. Moving slower on the tax increase or public employee collective bargaining, such critics contended, would have allowed more time to educate the public. Yet, in reality, the window of opportunity to advance on these fronts closed quickly. After controlling the Governor's office and both houses of the Legislature for two brief years, the Democrats lost their majority in the Senate in 1984. Riding on Ronald Reagan's coattails, the Republicans took control of the upper chamber by an eighteen-to-fifteen margin. Although Celeste would be re-elected in 1986 and the House would remain under Vern Riffe's gavel, the days of Democratic dominance were over. Tight party discipline by the GOP in the upper chamber stymied significant progressive legislative advances for the rest of the decade.

III

The Republicans also made gains in the Ohio Supreme Court, and at times held a majority, but by an odd twist of fate the Ohio AFL-CIO still retained considerable influence with the high tribunal. As we have seen, in the mid-1970s, the Ohio AFL-CIO escalated its involvement in state judicial races. As a consequence, for a decade the high court under the leadership of Chief Justice Frank Celebrezze made decisions in such areas as workers' compensation more in tune with the views of labor than those of management. In 1984, the victory of two Republicans in the Supreme Court race reduced the six-to-one Democratic majority to a four-to-three margin. However, one of the victorious Republicans was the maverick Andrew Douglas whose voting record on economic issues was closer to that of the Democratic Justices than to the stance taken by his fellow Republicans, and henceforth he received labor's endorsement.

Throughout 1984 and 1985 the Court continued issuing landmark rulings that expanded the coverage and rights of employees under the workers' compensation system. In the *Littlefield* decision the Court declared that an injury could be determined to be work-related if the worker 'but for' the employment would not have been where the accident took place and faced a much greater risk than the general public. In this particular case, Ronald Littlefield, an employee of the Pillsbury Company in Cincinnati working a twelve hour shift, had been required to work through both of his fifteen-minute breaks and his regular lunch period. When he finally was given time to eat, he drove to a restaurant less than a mile away since he did not have a bag meal for the plant lunchroom. On the way back, another car smashed his vehicle from behind as he was turning into the plant entrance and left him paralyzed. After lengthy litigation in which the Ohio AFL-CIO played a major role, the Supreme Court ruled that Littlefield was entitled to workers' compensation. Even though the accident occurred off company property, Pillsbury had set up the conditions that allowed it to occur.

The Ohio AFL-CIO took even greater delight in the Court's six-to-one decision in *Village vs. General Motors*. In this instance, the court overturned forty years of precedence and recognized the right of workers to receive workers' compensation for injuries developed gradually over a period of time, not just those injuries suffered as a result of a sudden and unexpected occurrence. Since the *Village* decision opened the possibility of greater state assistance to workers whose long-term employment had placed undue wear-and-tear on their bodies, *News and Views* felt it "could very well be the most important decision the Ohio Supreme Court has made concerning Ohio's workers' compensation law."

The state's business community also saw the import of decisions like *Littlefield* and *Village* and intensified its efforts to regain control of the Supreme Court. In the 1986 elections various corporate interests funded an intense attack by the Ohio State Bar Association on Chief Justice Frank Celebrezze, whom *News and Views* hailed as "the best friend workers have ever had on the bench." A victim of the most expensive campaign for the Court up to that date, Frank Celebrezze lost his bid for re-election and the Court returned to a four-to-three Republican majority. Yet, since Andrew Douglas continued his pro-worker stance, the Court remained sympathetic to labor on issues such as workers' compensation, much to the business community's chagrin.

In 1988, after a concerted effort by the Ohio AFL-CIO, the Democrats again regained a slim majority on the Court with the election of Alice Robie Resnick and the re-election of A. William Sweeney. The presence of a pro-worker majority on the Court literally saved the 1983 public employee collective bargaining law and protected the integrity of the worker's compensation system in 1983. That advantage, however, disappeared in 1990 when the GOP took two seats away from pro-labor Democrats.

Although the Democrats and Republicans engaged in hotly contested court races, both parties cooperated with the Ohio AFL-CIO in 1987 to preserve the system of electing judges. The Ohio Bar Association, embolden by its defeat of Chief Justice Frank Celebrezze in the 1986 elections, campaigned to amend the Ohio Constitution to eliminate the right of voters to choose Justices to the Ohio Supreme Court and the state's twelve District Courts of Appeal. The Bar Association's proposal, which became "Issue 3" on the November 1987 ballot, called for the Governor to appoint judges from a list of candidates selected by a panel composed half of attorneys and half of non-attorneys. Backed by banks, insurance firms, utility companies, and other interests upset with recent judicial decisions, the proponents of appointed judges spent over $2,000,000 in their campaign. Lacking comparable funds, the coalition of labor, farmer organizations, church groups, and the two political parties relied on grassroots mobilizing, which always had been the mainstay of the Ohio AFL-CIO's political action work. The strategy worked as the voters defeated Issue 3 by a two-to-one margin. "It was the second time in 50 years Ohio voters told the Bar Association and their corporate clients that they had no intention of giving up one of the most precious rights a free and open democratic society grants citizens," observed *News and Views* in its post-election edition. "Here's hoping the bar association and corporate Ohio were listening to what the voters were saying on Tuesday and keep this turkey penned up for another 50 years."

IV

Labor's political victories and defeats in the mid-1980s occurred at a time when the Ohio AFL-CIO suffered another internal leadership crisis. The original plan to have staff members cover for Secretary-Treasurer Warren Smith while he served in Celeste's cabinet proved unworkable. Smith was simply too busy heading the Department of Transportation to oversee effectively affairs at the State Street headquarters.

Nor was President Milan Marsh content with such

an arrangement. Previously, Marsh devoted much of his time to the Ohio State Council of Carpenters, for whom he served as Executive Secretary. With Smith on leave, however, Marsh moved into the vacuum. His autocratic and secretive style, along with the behavior of the personal entourage he recruited, polarized state headquarters. Increasingly, long-time staff members friendly with Warren Smith felt isolated. For instance, communications became so strained between Marsh and Community Services Director Charles Mix, a fellow carpenter, that Mix went into retirement in 1986.

Nor was Marsh effective in dealing with the General Assembly and Governor. In the mid-1980s, labor's lobbying clout weakened as ties to religious, civil rights, and other progressive groups withered. Less committed to coalition politics than earlier leaders, Marsh insisted that the Federation could achieve its legislative objectives on its own. Yet Marsh rarely met with legislators or testified at hearings, and the administrative assistant to whom he delegated legislative liaison proved ineffectual. The shortcomings of such an approach came home to roost in mid-May 1986, when the Ohio AFL-CIO failed to block, or at least modify, Senate Bill 307, which undermined recent pro-worker decisions by the Ohio Supreme Court. Marsh's stubborn refusal to explore compromise on a measure destined to pass resulted in the enactment of what *News and Views* declared to be "the most anti-worker bill since the introduction of right-to-work legislation in 1958."

Warren Smith recognized the turmoil on State Street, yet was hindered by his cabinet position from effectively intervening. Consequently, at the 15th Biennial Convention in June 1986, Smith formally relinquished the secretary-treasurership, allowing the delegates to elect someone able to devote all his/her energies to the post (and also setting the stage for his own eventual appointment by Governor Celeste to the Ohio Industrial Commission). True to his quiet nature, Smith spoke only briefly to the delegates, neither praising nor condemning Marsh. Rather, his parting comments invoked the past as he looked to the future. "Our history is not one that goes across the plateau," he mused, "our history is one of peaks and gullies, and we may be in a low valley right now, but our history proves that we will always come back . . . ."

Following the tradition of having a member of the largest affiliate to the Ohio AFL-CIO fill the post, the convention unanimously choose John Hodges of the United Steelworkers of America as the new Secretary-Treasurer. The son of a sharecropper, Hodges was born in January 1925, in rural North Carolina. The depression forced the family to move north with its six children to seek work in Ohio. In 1943, John left high school at the beginning of his senior year to join the Navy and fight in World War II. Hodges' union career began in 1947 when, as a new employee, he signed up with a union that was organizing the General Electric plant in Coshocton, Ohio. That union proved ineffectual, however, leading Hodges in 1950 to lead a successful campaign to decertify and install the Steelworkers in its place. He served as the new local's first President until 1959 when he became a staff representative for the Steelworkers. In 1973 he took over as Sub-District Director of the Steelworkers in Columbus. Shortly afterwards, he also assumed the duties as the President of the Columbus-Franklin County AFL-CIO.

Much to the disappointment of the Executive Board, the election of Hodges as Secretary-Treasurer did not bring calm to the Ohio AFL-CIO. On the contrary, over the next year increasing evidence emerged regarding Marsh's mismanagement of affairs. He disappeared from the state headquarters for three and four weeks at a time; ignored Hodges and long-serving staff representatives and dealt only with his hand picked assistants; and apparently billed his local union, the Ohio State Council of Carpenters, and the Ohio AFL-CIO all for the same trips. By late Summer 1987 most Executive Board members had concluded that the organization would best be served by Marsh's departure. Consequently, on September 25 they pressured him to step down as President. At a follow-up meeting on October 16, the members moved John Hodges to the top position in the Federation.

To fill the post of Secretary-Treasurer vacated by Hodges, the Board responded to the growing role of public sector unions and elected Donald Day from the American Federation of State, County, and Municipal Employees (AFSCME). Born in Cleveland in 1936, Day received his undergraduate degree from Kent State University and later did advanced studies at Harvard University's John F. Kennedy School of Government. Day's union career began as President of AFSCME Local 1746 in Cleveland. He later was elected President of AFSCME District 78 in northeast Ohio, Recording Secretary of the Cleveland AFL-CIO, and first Vice President of AFSCME Council 8 in Columbus. Over the years, Day had served on numerous boards advancing opportunities for minorities, providing better health care to the broader community, and making labor's presence felt in education and the fine arts. At the time of his election as Secretary-Treasurer he had served over a decade on the Executive Board.

V

Adhering to the old adage that new leadership, like a new broom, sweeps clean, the Ohio AFL-CIO underwent a house cleaning with the arrival of a new President and Secretary-Treasurer. Within days of taking office, Hodges fired Marsh's personal assistants. A few staff members took the occasion to move on, including Public Relations Director John Thomas, who was replaced by the respected newspaper reporter Kent Darr. Charles Mix reemerged from retirement to spearhead COPE and legislative affairs, and Patty Tutoki of IUE District 7 resigned from the Executive Board to become Director of Education and Safety. By late 1986, Larry Mitchell had become Comptroller when Ira Thompson retired. Finances drove some changes, such as the decision to suspend the publication of *Focus Quarterly*, while a belief in the effectiveness of graphics shaped the new format that editor Darr gave *News and Views*.

Hodges and Day also placed greater emphasis on providing unionists with a wide range of educational experiences. A labor dispute at Kenyon College in 1988 led the Ohio AFL-CIO to move the summer school, first to Kent State University, and then for the next half-dozen years to Ohio University. The shift in location brought renewed interest in the school, with over two hundred unionists in attendance at Kent State, eighty percent of them for the first time. Along with the summer school, the state organization revitalized the well-established conferences on civil rights, community service, and health and safety and added programming targeted at the growing number of women unionists. Donald Day took a special interest in reaching out to youth by working closely with Frontlash (the AFL-CIO's student organization) and by encouraging school children to observe the Federation's conventions.

A commitment to improve the educational offerings provided to the state's unionists also led John Hodges to play a leading role in re-organizing the workers' education program at The Ohio State University. For years, the Ohio AFL-CIO had successfully lobbied the General Assembly for funds for the University's Labor Education and Research Service (LERS). And for years, LERS had provided quality programming designed to improve labor relations in the state by closing the "knowledge gap" between management's college educated, full-time labor relations staff and organized labor's mostly unpaid, part-time local leadership, many of whom in the early years had not even finished high school.

By the late 1980s, though, what was needed in the area of labor programming had changed drastically from what had been called for several decades earlier. Over the years, the educational attainment of the average union member had advanced significantly, and a number of international unions had initiated their own schools and conferences to train rank-and-file leaders in basic skills. In light of these changes, Hodges felt that LERS ought to advance from offering routine courses on topics such as stewards training to researching the complex issues that confronted Ohio's working people and to disseminating the results throughout the state. Hodges' perspective coincided with that of University officials who increasingly questioned granting tenure and promotion to LERS staff members who failed to do research expected of faculty at a major university. Although some in LERS greeted the opportunity to focus more on scholarship, a larger group resisted the change and even unsuccessfully lobbied Executive Board members to pressure Hodges to relent. Instead the Board backed Hodges' plan to obtain the desired result through persuading the State Legislature to create a new Center for Labor Research (CLR). For two years the Ohio AFL-CIO lobbied the General Assembly for funding for both LERS and CLR while the University struggled to induce a shift to research within LERS. Finally, in July 1991, after Republicans in the General Assembly ended funding for LERS, the University abolished it as a tenure-initiating unit and transferred all labor programming activities to the Center for Labor Research.

VI

Hodges also revitalized the political lobbying of the Ohio AFL-CIO which had gone flat in the mid-1980s, in part because of Milan Marsh's style, but also because Governor Celeste sought business' favor over labor's political agenda. Now, with only two years left in his second term, the Governor began strengthening his ties with labor as a base for any future campaign for public office he might launch. The Ohio AFL-CIO met Celeste's receptiveness with a seven-point program which included raising the state minimum wage, upgrading unemployment compensation, and passing a "Little" Hatch Act to parallel the federal law that protected the right of public employees to engage in political activity. The Federation's agenda also called for extending health and safety safeguards to public employees, providing affordable childcare for all workers, mandating employers to provide healthcare, and reforming the state's Bureau of Workers' Compensation and Industrial Commission.

The Ohio AFL-CIO achieved reasonably quick success on a few issues, such as when the Legislature raised the state's minimum wage in June 1990. On a few other issues, victory came only after several years of lobbying, as when the 119th General Assembly, in one of its final acts, extended federal health and safety standards to nearly a half-million public workers. On other issues, most notably mandatory health care, victory did not come at all.

Foremost among Hodges' political objectives, however, was reform of the workers' compensation system. As a reasonable man, Hodges readily admitted that the system needed modernizing. He was acutely aware of workers waiting months and even years to have their claims processed and of medical costs that were out of control. Hodges also wanted to reverse some of the worse aspects of the legislation passed in 1985. After an audit in 1987 revealed a deficit that sent rates dramatically upward, the state's business community was also willing to consider reforming the system.

Informed by various public and private studies on the operation of the workers' compensation program, Hodges worked closely with business representatives in designing a new law to restructure the system and streamline the processing of claims. The legislation, which eventually became Amended Substitute House Bill 222, neither raised rates nor decreased premiums, but rather reorganized the Bureau of Workers' Compensation to operate more like an insurance company and reduced the role of the Industrial Commission to hearing contested claims. The measure created a board composed of four labor and four management representatives, along with four non-voting public officials, to oversee the Bureau and hire a director to manage the day-to-day affairs. The intent in creating the board was to decrease political influence on the Bureau by placing decision-making authority in the hands of those who knew the system best, the employers and workers who confronted it every day. As a "negotiated" bill supported by both labor and management, it passed the General Assembly with only minor dissent.

John Hodges, who in November 1989 became the first Chairman of the newly created Workers' Compensation Board, cheered the efforts to reorganize the system as "a major victory for working people." "The Ohio AFL-CIO entered into the task mindful that touching what many considered a sacred system would be a source of controversy both within and outside the labor movement," he reported to the delegates to the June 1990 convention. "But the system was in dire need of change, having evolved from a program designed to respond quickly to the financial and medical needs of injured workers to a system that was slowed by a cumbersome bureaucracy and had begun to serve the self-interests of political appointees." The new legislation, Hodges believed, allowed for better administration, improved computer record keeping, swifter appeals, and greater communication, the combination of which would produce notable improvements within a few years.

VII

If the workers' compensation reforms of 1989 represented one of the peaks Warren Smith had foreseen in his departing comments to the 1988 convention, then the November 1990 election commenced the descent into a gully. As in the past, the Ohio AFL-CIO went all out for the Democratic nominees, including Attorney General Anthony J. Celebreeze for Governor and State Senator Eugene Branstool for Lieutenant Governor. Yet labor's grass roots organizing could not overcome either Celebreeze's lackluster style or the financial resources of Cleveland Mayor George V. Voinovich, who emerged the victor in the most expensive gubernatorial campaign in Ohio history. Money alone, however, did not defeat labor and its candidates. A post-election study matching union rosters with the Secretary of State's records revealed that roughly forty percent of the state's union members were not registered to vote.

The election was doubly disastrous for the Ohio AFL-CIO. In the long run, the election turned control of the state's Apportionment Board over to the Republicans for the first time in twenty years. In the aftermath of both the 1970 and 1980 census, the Democrats held enough key positions to shape the apportionment process. Now the Republicans dominated the Board and when the 1990 census results came in they drew new district boundaries more in their favor. As a result of such gerrymandering, Republicans increased their majority in the state Senate and the Ohio Congressional delegation, and by mid-decade captured control of the Ohio House.

More immediately, the election placed in the Governor's office a man who packaged himself as a moderate, but who adopted the anti-union views of his chief financial backers affiliated with the Ohio Business Roundtable. Far more than his Republican predecessor James Rhodes, Voinovich had little positive to say about unions but rather attacked them as impediments to the economic development of the state. The Governor's famous chant to "do more with less" in part meant "less" union involvement in Ohio politics and policy. Despite constant efforts, which included the endorsements from such prominent Republicans as Chief Justice Thomas Moyer, John Hodges could not get an appointment to see the new Governor for almost a year. When he did get an audience, Hodges was immediately struck by Voinovich's extreme ego. According to Hodges, Voinovich spent this get-acquainted session fuming about how he was going to squeeze the state's university system dry and stonewalling any discussion on labor's immediate concerns.

The new Governor's assault on the labor movement and the causes it supported came quickly and remained persistent. Soon after the election, Governor-elect Voinovich glanced at the list of Celeste nominees for various appointments that were pending Senate confirmation — some waiting for as long as three years — and ordered the rejection of thirteen, eight of whom were from organized labor. Among them were the current Ohio AFL-CIO Secretary-Treasurer Donald K. Day, slated for the state's Ethics Commission, and the former Ohio AFL-CIO Secretary-Treasurer Warren J Smith who was already performing the duties of Chairman of the Industrial Commission.

On the legislative front, Voinovich advanced proposals guaranteed to raise labor's ire. He sought to privatize the state's liquor stores, thus eliminating good paying union jobs. Another proposal authorized a mandatory deposit on beverage containers much like the "bottle bill" initiative that the Ohio AFL-CIO helped defeat in 1979. And still a third measure radically reduced the state-financed General Assistance Welfare Program for "able-bodied" adults with no children. More directly attacking the labor movement, Voinovich used the guise of campaign finance reform to seek legislation restricting union contributions to political candidates. He even attacked those unions in the building trades that traditionally supported Republicans by suggesting modifications of the prevailing wage laws to exempt a wide range of government-funded construction.

Voinovich released his most vigorous attack, however, on the workers' compensation system, which ironically was in the midst of reforming itself under the 1989 reorganization legislation. Wanting to assert his personal influence over all aspects of government, from the state school board on down, Voinovich disliked the 1989 reform bill's efforts to de-politicize the workers' compensation system. Encouraging Voinovich's effort to change the system were the businessmen who had backed his campaign and were affiliated with the Ohio Business Roundtable. Such individuals found the often-unanimous decisions coming out of the Workers' Compensation Board troublesome as they did little to decrease their premiums. Some business leaders even thought the system would better meet their needs if it were privatized. On January 17, 1991, within days of taking office, Governor Voinovich told the Greater Cleveland Growth Association that Workers' Compensation was "the most negative thing hurting business in the State of Ohio, and we got to change it now." He was even more direct when talking to local government officials, business representatives, and school officials at an education summit on January 22. "It's the worst problem facing local government, schools and business in this state. Money is going into workers' compensation that should be going into providing services for our citizens." Soon he had his criticism of the system down to a chant: “Make no mistake about it — our workers’ compensation system is the silent killer of jobs in Ohio!”

Thus, whereas Hodges had spent the first two years of his presidency working within the conducive climate of the Celeste administration, he spent the remaining years trying to put out the fires started by Voinovich. With the help of a Democratic majority in the Ohio House in 1991 and 1992, he successfully stymied or slowed most of the Governor’s initiatives that labor opposed and even won health and safety coverage for state employees. The 1992 elections, however, further weakened the Democratic majority in the House and gave heart to Voinovich and Republican legislators to push harder on their agenda. Increasingly the workers’ compensation system became the center of controversy. Through a skillful campaign to mobilize public opinion and through cunning legislative maneuvering, Amended Substitute House Bill 107 passed the General Assembly and was signed into law on July 20, 1993. A rally of nearly 1,000 unionists staged by the Ohio AFL-CIO only a few days before passage of the bill helped convince the Legislative Conference Committee not to eliminate or reduce benefits received by injured workers. Still, Hodges viewed the legislation as a terrible setback. “This is the worst defeat for working people in the history of workers’ compensation in Ohio,” he told reporters. And with clear perception, he warned, “The Chamber of Commerce, Ohio Manufacturers’ Association, the Ohio Business Roundtable and the insurance industry are circling like buzzards over this system and they are going to pick it apart a piece at a time.”

Hodges, however, would not be leading the Ohio AFL-CIO in resisting the future assaults on the workers’ compensation system. At sixty-eight, Hodges felt the time had come for him to retire and pass the reigns of leadership to the next generation. He had served the labor movement admirably for over forty-five years, six of them as President of the Federation. During those years, his accomplishments were many, but foremost among them was reestablishing the integrity of the organization and its ties to working men and women around the state.

Ohio AFL-CIO President Frank King speaks at the 1968 Democratic National Convention in Chicago. (Ohio AFL-CIO Collection at the Ohio Historical Society)

Frank King (center) helps John J. Gilligan's (right) campaign for the U.S. Senate in 1968. (Ohio AFL-CIO Collection at the Ohio Historical Society)

Frank King, Ohio AFL-CIO Secretary-Treasurer Warren Smith, and Gilligan sharing the podium at an Ohio AFL-CIO conference. (Ohio AFL-CIO Collection at the Ohio Historical Society)

Gubernatorial candidate John Gilligan confers with King during a 1970 campaign rally. (Ohio AFL-CIO Collection at the Ohio Historical Society)

Ohio AFL-CIO President Milan Marsh greets presidential hopeful Edward Kennedy at the 1980 Biennial Convention. (Ohio AFL-CIO)

Ohio AFL-CIO President John Hodges addresses a labor crowd, while Secretary-Treasurer Donald Day prepares to talk. (Ohio AFL-CIO)

Hodges and his wife Almena pose with Governor Richard Celeste. (Photo courtesy of John Hodges)

Hodges meets with presidential candidate Bill Clinton during the 1992 campaign. (Photo courtesy of John Hodges)

Chapter Seven

An Unfinished Chapter, 1994-1998

I

On October 29, 1993, the Ohio AFL-CIO Executive Board elected William A. Burga to complete the term of retiring President John R. Hodges. Eight months later, at the June 1994 Convention, the delegates elected Burga by acclimation to a full four-year term, as well as re-elected Donald Day as Secretary-Treasurer and forty Vice-Presidents. For only the second time in the Ohio AFL-CIO's thirty-six year history the delegates had supported the entire leadership slate on the first ballot.

Bill Burga, the Ohio AFL-CIO's seventh President, was born in Bethesda, Belmont County, Ohio in 1936. At eighteen he went to work for the Timken Company, but moved on to the Jones and Laughlin Steel Corporation's Louisville, Ohio, plant a few years later. In 1959, Burga helped organize that facility under the banner of the United Steelworkers of America and began his rise in union offices, first as a Grievance Committeeman, then local Treasurer, and from 1964 to 1969 as local President. During these years he was also elected to several offices in the Greater Canton AFL-CIO. In 1969 the Steelworkers appointed Burga to the international staff and assigned him to the Marion-Mansfield area. Along with attending to the area's steelworkers, Burga served as President of the Marion County AFL-CIO from 1972 to 1982. In October 1984, Burga became Director of the Steelworkers' Sub-District in Canton. And again, Burga got into the thick of central body affairs, serving as President of the Massillon Trades and Labor Council from 1987 until his election as President of the Ohio AFL-CIO. Along with grassroots experience in the Steelworkers and extensive participation in three different central bodies, Burga brought to the presidency of the Ohio AFL-CIO a long-running involvement in both the state and national Democratic Party. He had been an alternate to the 1976 Democratic National Convention and a delegate to the convention in 1984. As President of the Ohio AFL-CIO he would become a member of the Democratic National Committee and the Ohio Democratic Party Executive Committee. He would also be a delegate to the 1996 Democratic National Convention where he gave one of the more impressive on-camera interviews on the dangers of the Republican's national agenda.

Burga's background and experience clearly shaped his approach to the presidency and his agenda for the Ohio AFL-CIO. Two years before John Sweeney took the helm of the national AFL-CIO on a platform calling for a rejuvenation of labor, Burga commenced preaching the gospel of grassroots involvement, improved communications, broader coalitions, and proactive politics. As soon as he became Ohio AFL-CIO President, he set out to strengthen the Federation's ties to the central bodies. Amid a hectic schedule during his first two years in office, Burga managed to visit half of the state's then forty-four labor councils. Moreover, with Charlie Mix retiring when Hodges stepped down, in early 1994 Burga recruited to state headquarters David L. Kolbe of Iron Workers Local 55, who brought with him a rich experience in both labor and Democratic Party affairs in northwest Ohio. Along with coordinating legislation and COPE operations, Kolbe acted as a liaison between the Ohio AFL-CIO and the central bodies. A few months later, in May 1994, the Ohio AFL-CIO adopted new COPE by-laws for endorsing candidates that gave central bodies more voice in the process.

In another step to strengthen ties with rank-and-file unionists, Burga revised the organization's methods of communicating. *News and Views* underwent another format change to make it more appealing to its readership. Additionally, in January 1994, the organization began sending a monthly video to the central bodies for showing at meetings. The first edition of the video newsletter featured information on health care reform and comments from Ohio Senator Robert Burch on his plans to challenge Voinovich for Governor in the fall. The February 1994 edition contained remarks from Joel Hyatt, labor's endorsed candidate for the U.S. Senate, and information on the North America Free Trade Act job loss assistance program. In another innovation, the Ohio AFL-CIO launched the Ohio Worker's Radio Network, which by September 1995, broadcasted a special weekly labor show over nine stations across the state. Finally, Communications Director Kent Darr took particular delight in introducing on Labor Day 1995 the Ohio AFL-CIO WORKBOX, a very polished World Wide Web page that conveyed the most up-to-date information on legislation, labor disputes, and other developments. The web, moreover, opened the door for a two-way flow of information, as local affiliates and rank-and-file members could communicate by e-mail directly with the Columbus office.

Yet for Burga, no amount of electronic wizardry could replace the value of face-to-face contracts. When not out in the field visiting union halls, he was hosting groups in Columbus. Long running programs like the Workers' Compensation Institute and the Civil Rights/ Women in Leadership Development Conferences continued to attract large crowds. Attendance also remained vigorous at the annual summer school, which was moved from Ohio University to The Ohio State University in 1995, and then to Kenyon College in 1996. Because of a labor dispute at Kenyon College in 1997, however, the state body canceled the program that year to avoid violating picket lines.

Most importantly, in March 1995, the state body held its first Legislative Conference in fourteen years. As part of the conference, over 1,000 unionists marched to the state capital to lobby lawmakers on a range of bills. Rallies are a major element in Burga's strategy to communicate with workers and to have them lobby legislators. For instance, on November 4, 1995, over 20,000 trade unionists braced cold temperatures and strong winds to hear Bill Burga, Donald Day, and national AFL-CIO Secretary-Treasurer Richard Trumka lambaste Republican legislators for their assault on prevailing wage, public employee collective bargaining rights, and a range of family issues.

Along with involving more members in state body activities, Burga has also sought to increase the number of Ohio unionists formally affiliated with the Ohio AFL-CIO. To do so, he recruited Larry "Lefty" Sanders of the Firefighters to get "free-riding" locals to affiliate with the state body and to get those affiliates that under-report their membership to pay in full. Sanders has also worked to convince internationals to take advantage of a national AFL-CIO rule that allows them to pay the Federation for all their members in the state at 75 percent of the per capita tax rate. Only three affiliated international unions, however, provide payment to the Ohio AFL-CIO in this manner. Still, success is being made on the affiliation front, with 20,363 new members being recruited between 1995 and 1996 alone.

Finally, the Ohio AFL-CIO has continued to aggressively build bridges with allies outside the labor movement. Historic ties to civil rights, civic, and farm organizations have been strengthened and new ties with groups like the trial lawyers have been built. Burga has taken a personal interest in linking up with churches by establishing Labor-Religion Councils around the state. The Federation has also stimulated the organization of retiree councils in the major metropolitan centers. These councils held their first statewide conference in September 1996 and attained affiliate standing with the state body.

II

The legislative attack on both unions and workers continued unabated in the mid-1990s, and, indeed, became more intense once the Republicans gained control of the Ohio House in 1994, thus giving them complete sway over the General Assembly and the Governor's office. Yet while battling with hostile legislators and the Governor, Bill Burga remained mindful that the real power behind the scene was the business interests in the state. "The reality of all of this . . . ," he reminded readers of *News & Views* in September 1995, "is that it is not the government we should be worried so much about, but the corporations. It is the corporations that the Republicans listen to. Corporations have always fought workers' rights and unions; they have never accepted us and they never will. The problem now is that the Republicans in public office are unified almost to a person in lockstep with corporations in this country."

With attorneys for various business associations busy plotting legislation for Republican solons to introduce, the Ohio Manufacturers Association *News* in July 1995 praised the 121st General Assembly as "the most pro-manufacturing legislature to convene in Columbus in more than 20 years." To sooth agribusiness, lawmakers passed bills protecting cows and lettuce from slander, yet they seriously limited workers' ability to collect damages when they are intentionally injured on the job. Likewise, the lawmakers limited a workers ability to get redress when a boss provides a malicious job evaluation to another potential employer. The 121st General Assembly also weakened the Public Employees Occupational Safety and Health law, prohibited partial strikes by public workers, and eliminated prevailing wage on state printing contracts. Finally, striking directly at unions, the General Assembly also passed Senate Bill 8 that limited labor's political contributions.

The Ohio AFL-CIO's strenuous efforts in the 1996 election were not successful in slowing the anti-worker, anti-union juggernaut. Labor's allies were in short supply in the 122nd General Assembly which convened in January 1997, with Republicans dominating the House sixty to thirty-nine and controlling the Senate twenty-one to twelve. Under the guise of solving a school-funding crisis, Republican legislators eliminated the prevailing wage requirement on school construction projects. Over 3,000 union construction workers, many of who had previously supported Republicans, descended on Columbus during the final debate on the bill in hope of turning the legislative tide. But instead of a sympathetic hearing, the construction workers received a lecture from Senator Nancy Chiles Dix on their being "ridiculously over paid." To punish the labor movement for protesting the elimination of prevailing wage, the legislators abolished funding for OSU's Center for Labor Research, thus ending (at least temporarily) three decades of state funding for workers' education.

From the beginning of his presidency, Burga toyed with the idea of finding some statewide ballot issue to re-invigorate the labor movement, much as the fights over right-to-work and reapportionment had done years earlier. In February 1994, he had mused that the issue might be the attempt by business and Republicans to scale back the right of unions to engage in political action. "This may be the issue we need to have the pendulum swing back to support workers' rights and restore balance of power in government to the people over selfish, business interests," he wrote in *News & Views*. But the time was not right in 1994 for such a move. Before launching such a battle, Burga's plan for energizing the state labor movement through improved communications, stronger ties to the grass roots and central labor bodies, and coalition building had to be put in place.

By early 1997, the Ohio AFL-CIO was prepared and the need for such a fight was all the more urgent. Moreover the issue to be contested was crystal clear.

Since 1990, at the business community's bidding, the Voinovich administration had fought unceasingly to weaken the workers' compensation system. No sooner had pro-business reforms of the system been passed in 1993 than the Ohio Manufacturers Association and the Ohio Business Roundtable, masquerading under the name Citizens for Responsible Workers' Compensation Reform, launched a $400,000 publicity campaign to pave the way for further cutbacks in the program. This effort came to fruition in Senate Bill 45, which was signed into law by Governor Voinovich on April 22, 1997, to take effect on July 22. The overall effect of the new law would be to transfer roughly $200 million annually from workers (in the form of benefits) to businesses (in the form of reduced premium payments). For labor the most objectionable of the law's provisions were those that cut nonworking wage loss benefits by eighty-seven percent, shortened case life to five from ten years, made it more difficult to prove carpal-tunnel syndrome, and allowed firms to keep safety violations secret.

The Ohio AFL-CIO could not have found a better issue on which to challenge the corporate/Republican anti-worker drive had it written it itself. First, in defending the integrity of the workers' compensation system the Ohio AFL-CIO was protecting the interests of all workers, whether union or nonunion, professional or unskilled, well paid or minimum wage. Second, the state body had long recognized workers' compensation as the flip side of workplace safety and skillfully communicated that connection to the general public. Third, the fight over Senate Bill 45 flushed corporate interests out into the open, revealing to the public that the bill's major financial supporters — Ford, GM, Proctor & Gamble, Bank One, Ohio Health Care, Timken — stood to gain by retaining the law. And finally, strategically the November 1997 ballot was perfect since it was free of other hotly contested statewide issues or candidates.

Thus, when the Academy of Trail Lawyers approached Bill Burga and Warren Davis of the UAW about challenging Senate Bill 45 through the referendum process, Burga readily secured the approval of the Ohio AFL-CIO Executive Board. Along with the trial lawyers and advocate groups for injured workers, the Ohio AFL-CIO and the UAW organized the Coalition for Workplace Safety to gain the 200,000 signatures needed by mid-July to get the referendum on the ballot. To the surprise of almost everyone, in mid-July the Coalition turned over to the Secretary of State more than twice the number of needed signatures. Thus the referendum on Senate Bill 45 became Issue 2 on the November ballot, with the proposition strategically worded that opponents of the law had to vote "no."

Business groups and their Republican allies picked up on Governor Voinovich's lament that workers' compensation was the "killer of jobs in Ohio" and labeled their front organization Keep Ohio Working. In contrast, the Ohio AFL-CIO expanded its coalition to include farm, civil rights, and religious groups under the umbrella of the Committee to Stop Corporate Attacks on Injured Workers. Keep Ohio Working had the greater financial resources — in the end it spent three times as much as its opponents — and relied heavily on television advertisements and Voinovich's popularity to carry its case. Labor and its allies, however, worked at the grassroots level.

Long experienced in elections, the Ohio AFL-CIO knew that the key to victory lay in union members' hands. In preliminary planning, the Federation's leadership predicted a forty-five percent voter turnout, with only forty-five percent of the general public voting 'no' on Issue 2. To triumph, the Ohio AFL-CIO figured that it had "to get 55% of our labor households to the polls and to persuade at least 70% of them to vote No on Issue 2." Thus, with limited resources, the Ohio AFL-CIO and coalition unions launched a two-pronged campaign. First, they mobilized unionists through direct mailings, newsletters, and phone banks, and, second, they sought to counterbalance Keep Ohio Working's media blitz.

The shrewd campaign strategy worked. Although by mid-October the state's newspapers were seduced by Keep Ohio Working's media campaign and their own prejudices into predicting a business triumph, labor and its allies smelled a victory. Polls from across the state indicated that despite an expensive advertising campaign by pro-Issue 2 forces, most Ohioans remained undecided. And then by Halloween, labor's grassroots strategy began to sprout. "A forest of 100,000 green 'Vote No on 2' yard signs bloomed across the state's urban and rural areas," noted the *People's Weekly World*. "Hundreds of thousands of fliers reached into the grass-roots, and 360,000 absentee ballots were put into the hands of union retirees." The state leadership had done well in conveying the importance of Issue 2 to the rank-and-file, who, in turn, educated their non-union neighbors.

The genuineness of that grassroots involvement was epitomized by an unknown unionist who stood from dawn to dark in front of a polling place in the Clintonville section of Columbus. Despite the drizzling rain, for fourteen hours he cheerfully greeted voters and asked for their support. Peppy and good-humored, his dedication and upbeat demeanor left no doubt that this was to be labor's day. And it was: Issue 2 went down to defeat by an astounding fifty-seven to forty-three margin.

III

On Saturday, February 7, 1998, three months following the victory on Issue 2, the Ohio AFL-CIO convened a special convention in Columbus. The glow of the November victory still lingered as the thousand delegates projected a positive, confident, upbeat mood. But the delegates' attention focused more on the future than the past. The concern of all was to keep the momentum going to ensure political victories into the November elections. At stake were both the election of state officials and control of the reapportionment process for a decade to come.

With unanimity, the delegates approved a "Bill of Rights" that called on government to guarantee each Ohioan a safe and secure retirement; a living wage and equal pay; adequate, affordable health care; a prevailing wage, a secure job, equal access to job opportunities/ affirmative action; safe work place; high quality public education; and the right to organize and be represented by a union. The delegates also voted in place a campaign strategy to elect officials committed to labor's program, and to add muscle to their efforts, the delegates approved the first dues increase for the state body in eighteen years.

In all, it was a business-like gathering with few histrionics and no dissent. All present had been down the road before. Experienced unionists, they knew they were fighters in an unceasing struggle to better the lives of working people. They understood politics as an ongoing contest of interests, with no issue permanently settled.

With the fortieth anniversary of the Ohio AFL-CIO near and the November elections ahead, the delegates and leaders left the special convention still participants in an unfinished chapter which will require dedication, hard work, and good fortune to bring to a successful conclusion.

Trade unionists attending a 1995 Ohio AFL-CIO legislative conference march to the Statehouse. (Ohio AFL-CIO)

Ohio AFL-CIO Secretary-Treasurer Donald Day speaks to Akron city workers in 1997. (Ohio AFL-CIO)

Ohio AFL-CIO President William A. Burga and Donald Day meet with national AFL-CIO Secretary-Treasurer Richard Trumka at the 1995 legislative conference. (Ohio AFL-CIO)

William Burga illustrates a point to United States Secretary of Commerce Ronald Brown at the Midwest Economic Summit chaired by President Clinton in 1995. (Ohio AFL-CIO)

Trade unionists march through downtown Columbus hoping to convince Ohio voters to defeat Issue 2, the 1997 business-sponsored initiative to curtail Workers' Compensation benefits. (Ohio AFL-CIO)

William Burga leading anti-Issue 2 unionists on the Statehouse lawn. (Ohio AFL-CIO)

1998 gubernatorial candidate Lee Fisher removes his coat to show off his Ohio AFL-CIO t-shirt at the 1998 Special Convention. (Ohio AFL-CIO)

William Burga and George Becker, USWA President, share the podium with national AFL-CIO President John Sweeney. (Ohio AFL-CIO)

CONCLUSION

Over its forty year history, the Ohio AFL-CIO has been one of the most significant forces in the political affairs of the Buckeye State. As the foregoing pages attest, however, a range of factors has constantly interacted to shape the ability of the Federation to accomplish its political goals at any historical moment. Over the years the most important of these factors have been the general political culture of the state; broad social, economic, and political events over which the organization had little influence; the peculiarities of individual elections and candidates; and the character of the state body's leadership and the tranquility of its internal affairs. The actual goals of the Federation, however, have remained rather consistent over time.

Since its founding in 1958, the Ohio AFL-CIO's activities in the political arena have basically fallen into four categories. First, the Federation has concentrated on self-preservation, without which all other efforts would be meaningless. From the start, Federation leaders understood that government played a major role in making or breaking labor. If the General Assembly passes legislation to weaken unions or limit their effectiveness, then workers would lose a voice in the political process. For in contemporary America, government is negotiated through organizations such as the Chamber of Commerce, the National Association of Manufacturers, and the American Medical Association. Average Ohioans, to have their interests protected, need organizations such as the Ohio AFL-CIO engaged in politics for them. Thus, to maintain its right to exist and have an influence, over the years the Ohio AFL-CIO has resisted efforts to curtail its activities — from challenging the Right to Work amendment in 1958 to opposing current bills limiting union contributions to political campaigns. The Ohio AFL-CIO also fought hard for a quarter of a century to win a 1983 law granting public employees collective bargaining rights. In a society where government is the largest single employer, the Ohio AFL-CIO won for public sector workers many of the same rights guaranteed those laboring in private industry fifty years earlier.

The second category of issues on which the Ohio AFL-CIO has worked over the years is those that are clearly job related. Workplace safety is high on the list. In the 1970s, the Ohio AFL-CIO stood in the vanguard of groups promoting better state enforcement of the Occupational Safety and Health Act. During the late 1980s and early 1990s it led the battle in the state Legislature for a law that extends to public employees similar safety and health protection as granted to workers in the private sector. To promote safety in what has become one of the most dangerous jobs in America, highway construction, the Ohio AFL-CIO backed recent legislation doubling fines for speeding through highway construction zones. The Federation also has engaged in an unending struggle maintaining the integrity of the state's Workers' Compensation and Unemployment Insurance programs. Without the monitoring of the Ohio AFL-CIO, employers and their legislative allies would have cut back these programs to barebone, providing little protection to union and non-union workers injured or laid-off of a job. There have been a host of other job related issues that demanded the political attention of the Ohio AFL-CIO, from establishing and advancing a state minimum wage for those workers — truly marginal—not covered by the federal minimum standards to establishing standards to protect Ohio's migratory farm workers.

The third category of issues that the Ohio AFL-CIO has advanced have been measures to make the governmental process more democratic and accessible. In 1960 the Ohio AFL-CIO tried to change the election law to make election day a legal holiday and to keep the polls open until 8:00 pm. One of the most prolonged struggles began in the mid-1960s when the U.S. Supreme Court issued its one-person one-vote decision that required State Legislatures to be apportioned to roughly equal representation. Since the turn of the century Ohio's rural counties had been grossly overrepresented in the state assembly. As part of this battle for fair representation, in 1965 the Ohio AFL-CIO successfully led an all out drive to defeat a Republican-skewed reapportionment ballot issue. In the 1970s, the State Federation supported lowering the age of voting to eighteen and campaigned to liberalize voter registration laws so that the widest number of people could participate in the political process.

One form of democratization that the Ohio AFL-CIO has spent considerable time pushing over the last forty years has been tax reform. The Federation's activities have moved in two directions. First, the Federation has been lobbying the state to move away from a regressive tax system based on sales and personal property, which hits working families hardest, toward a progressive tax system based on income and wealth. Thus, the organization took the lead in the early 1970s in defending the state's income tax. Secondly, the Ohio AFL-CIO has insisted that the state develop the needed revenue base to provide the social and educational programming needed by its citizenry.

The fourth area of focus for the Ohio AFL-CIO has been advancing the general welfare of the average Ohioan, regardless of union membership. The issues included in this category run an extremely wide gamut. In the 1960s, the state body was a major endorser of Governor Rhodes' program to make vocational and technical training more readily available in the state. In the 1970s, the organization spent considerable time seeking to improve regulation of auto insurance companies. In the 1980s, the Federation was at the forefront of those wanting the state to underwrite low interest mortgages for low and moderate income Ohioans. And in the 1990s the Ohio AFL-CIO fought for more accessible health care and a more equitable school funding program.

These then are the four fronts on which the Ohio AFL-CIO has labored — self-preservation, job-connected issues, democratization of the political process, and general issues for the common good. The struggle has put the Federation in the halls of the Legislature. But the organization has also frequently had to go into the courts. And it is always working the elections. More often than not organized labor has supported Democrats over Republicans — but not exclusively. But even with the people it opposed, it always searched for some common ground. And this is perhaps why its record of success in the four arenas is so uneven.

The Ohio AFL-CIO's record of achieving its program over the last forty years has been mixed. It has met with the least success on those issues dealing with self-preservation. On these issues labor's special needs are high and its links to allies are low. The current attack on prevailing wage is one that the organization is having great difficulty in gaining supporters to oppose. On the other hand, labor has had the greatest success in advancing its broader community-based agenda because it has been able to attract the widest range of supporters — from business, community, religious, civil rights, and other groups.

Any final assessment of the role of the Ohio AFL-CIO in Ohio affairs must end up concluding that it has been the backbone of whatever progressive change has occurred over the past. It might not have been on the cutting edge of all issues, but when it hooked up on those issues, things changed. As a unionist informed the authors when they began their research: "I can guarantee you that you will end up admiring us, at times even despite ourselves."

APPENDIX A

Presidents and Secretary-Treasurers

President

Michael Lyden (Youngstown, Transit Workers) 1958-1960
Phillip Hannah (Cleveland, International Association of Machinists) 1960-1962
David Kane (Dayton, Bookbinders) 1962-1964
Frank King (Toledo, Bricklayers and Teachers) 1964-1974
Milan Marsh (Youngstown, Carpenters) 1974-1987
John Hodges (Columbus, Steelworkers) 1987-1993
William Burga (Canton, Steelworkers) 1993-present

Executive Vice President

Phillip Hannah (Cleveland, International Association of Machinists) 1958-1960

Secretary-Treasurer

Elmer Cope (Warren, Steelworkers) 1958-1963
Robert Bollard (Cincinnati, Steelworkers) 1963-1967
Warren Smith (Lima, Steelworkers) 1967-1986
John Hodges (Columbus , Steelworkers) 1986-1987
Donald Day (Cleveland , AFSCME) 1987-present

APPENDIX B

Ohio AFL-CIO Executive Board Members

Acton, Richard D.	IBEW	1974–present
Alexander, Clyde	Glass & Ceramic	1974–1982
Alexander, Ronald C.	AFSCME/OCSEA	1987–present
Amdur, Max	ACTWU	1960–1962 1964–1966 1968–1979
Arconti, Thomas	Hod Carriers	1958–1960
Bachmann, Carl A.	Oil, Chemical & Atomic	1968–1981
Baker, Edgar E.	Bricklayers	1958–1963
Ballard, Charles	UAW	1958–1965
Bartlett, John	UFCW	1986–1989
Beckes, Michael E.	Carpenters	1981–1994
Bell, Sandra	AFSCME/OCSEA	1996–present
Berroyer, Rebecca	UFCW	1996–present
Bilik, Al	AFSCME	1968–1969
Bindas, Michael	IUE	1988–present
Bodi, Edward	UAW	1965–1968
Boehnlein, Philip	GCIU	1990–1994
Bowen, Jim	USWA	1986–1996
Brant, Verne	IUE	1976–1978
Bratka, Jon	RWDSU	1990–1995
Brindza, Robert A.	AFSCME	1983–1992
Buchanan, Robert P.	Oil, Chemical & Atomic	1960–1962 1966–1967
Burton, Charles L.	Fire Fighters	1970–1974
Bussa, Homer	USWA	1966–1975

Ohio AFL-CIO Executive Board Members (continued)

Cimino, Frank	UFCW	1978–1986
Clark, Elwood	AFSCME/OCSEA	1995–1996
Coggins Jr., Edward	Utility Workers	1973–1991
Comer, William A.	Utility Workers	1968-1973
Cook, Arthur R.	Upholsterers	1962–1974
Coyle, Joseph	USWA	1984–1990
Crellin, William R.	Plumbers & Pipefitters	1983–1990
Davis, Clarence	IAM	1995–1996
Day, Donald	AFSCME	1974–1987
Dean, Summers	USWA	1975–1977
Dean Jr., Robert H.	Oil, Chemical & Atomic	1981–1995
DeCresce, Larry	AFSCME/OAPSE	1988–1988
DeMore, Matthew	IAM	1958–1962
Ditmer, Dodie	CWA	1994–present
Dominico, David A.	Laborers	1990–1994
Donahue, Mickey	Plumbers & Pipefitters	1972–1974
Dougherty, Harry O.	USWA	1970–1972
Dugan, Leo E.	URW	1958–1973
Dunlap, Cecil B.	Retail Clerks	1962–1966
Easterling, Barbara J.	CWA	1974–1990
Edmonds, James W.	Textile Workers	1964–1966
Endsley, William	AFSCME	1994–present
Entinger, Jacob H.	USWA	1977–1982
Erdos, Harold	Mine Workers	1996–present
Erwin, Earl A.	Operating Engineers	1978–1983
Ewing, William E.	RWDSU	1980–1986
Fada, Robert	GMP	1990–present
Farrington, Robert Y.	Building Trades	1984–1997
Ferguson, J. Earl	Lathers	1962–1966

Ohio AFL-CIO Executive Board Members (continued)

Ferline, Jack	USWA	1970–1978
Finegan, William	Stage Employees	1958–1962
Fire, Edward	IUE	1970–1983
Fitzmaurice, David J.	IUE	1960–1966 1968–1969
Frisbee, Thomas D.	IAM	1996–present
Fulimeni, Tino	USWA	1994–present
Gallagher, James P.	USWA	1960–1962 1964–1966 1968–1970
Gannon, John	Fire Fighters	1970–1974
Gassman, Erwin J.	Typographic	1970–1988
Gembus, Joseph	Glass & Ceramic	1958–1974
Glaserman, Marty	SEIU	1994–1997
Goldberg, William	Carpenters	1958–1962
Graham, Martin F.	Bricklayers	1963–1970
Griffin, James P.	USWA	1960–1962 1964–1966 1968–1970
Haas, Ralph R.	Plumbers & Pipefitters	1970–1972
Hall, Ernest J.	Oil, Chemical & Atomic	1967–1968
Hendershott, Kenneth	Paperworkers	1968–1974
Hennigin, George	UFCW	1989–1993
Herman, Wayne R.	Molders	1974–1982
Hetrick, Lisa	SEIU	1996–present
Higgenbottam-Thompson, Marie	CWA	1990–1994
Holland, Gerald	Fire Fighters	1982–1994
Hornbeck, Clarence	Alum., Brick & Glass	1997–present
Hostetter, H. Victor	IAM	1978–1990

Ohio AFL-CIO Executive Board Members (continued)

Hughes, Gerald A.	RWDSU	1964–1966
		1968–1980
Hughes, Martin J.	CWA	1958–1962
		1964–1971
		1972–1988
Humphreys, James	IUE	1972–1974
Iafelice, James	IAM	1965–1974
Jackson, Amos	Laborers	1962–1990
Jamison, Carroll	Meat Cutters	1964–1978
Janis, Sam	ILGWU	1974–1978
Jeffries, James J.	Oil, Chemical & Atomic	1995–present
Jennings, Leo	UFCW	1995–1995
Jerele, Jim	UFCW	1991–present
Johns, John S.	USWA	1958–1973
Johnson, Robert	CWA	1988–1994
Johnston, Gerald P.	Paperworkers	1995–present
Katzler, Jack	Brewery Workers	1966–1968
Keller, James P.	Utility Workers	1995–present
King Sr., Wayne L.	GMP	1988–1997
Kistemaker, Arthur P.	Hod Carriers	1958–1964
Klopp, Robert	Building Trades	1970–1972
Kolkman, Eugene	UFCW	1991–1996
Konyha, William	Carpenters	1964–1972
Kott, Joseph	IAM	1964–1965
Lawniczak, James	Alum., Brick & Glass	1992–1997
Leseganich, Frank	USWA	1970–1982
Lester, Harry E.	USWA	1984–1995
Lewis, Ray	USWA	1990–present
Lorenzetti, Ralph J.	UFCW	1977–1991
Louttit, Richard C.	USWA	1990–present

Ohio AFL-CIO Executive Board Members (continued)

Lupica, Sebastian	Painters	1958–1962 1964–1974
Lynsky, Mark	Laborers	1994–1996
Madzelonka, Joseph	UFCW	1978–1990
Magi, Aldo	Paperworkers	1962–1964
Magyar, Anthony J.	ACTWU	1974–1982
Makoski, Chester	ACTWU	1979–1998
Marec, Ronald	Ohio Fed. of Teachers	1978–present
Martin, Dan	USWA	1990–present
Martin, Gary	AFSCME/OAPSE	1994–present
Mayfield, Harry E.	USWA	1973–1984
McBennett, John	Utility Workers	1964–1966
McDonald, David	UFCW	1966–1978
McDonald, Thomas E.	Iron Workers	1958–1970
McNamara, Frank	Carpenters	1972–1981
Meccia, Marco	Clothing Workers	1959–1960
Moore, John	RWDSU	1995–present
Morgan, Thomas E.	AFSCME	1969–1983
Moss, Patricia	AFSCME	1992–present
Motsinger, Genevieve	IUE	1974–1981
Mullahy, Joseph	Plumbers & Pipefitters	1958–1962
Murphy, Joseph	SEIU	1962–1964 1968–1970
Murphy, Michael	SEIU	1997–present
Murphy, Robert	Utility Workers	1958–1964
Nardella, John	URW	1982–1990
Nichols, Harold	IUE	1989–present
Null Sr., Lester H.	Pottery Workers	1974–1988
O'Malley, Patrick J.	UAW	1958–1968
Ocheske, Roy N.	Alum., Brick & Glass	1982–1992

Ohio AFL-CIO Executive Board Members (continued)

Pancake, Charles L.	IBEW	1966–1974
Peterson, Carl W.	Oil, Chemical & Atomic	1960–1960
Pinzone, Charles R.	Building Trades	1971–1974
Potter, Gene A.	Utility Workers	1991–1995
Radabaugh, Lawrence W.	Retail Clerks	1960–1964
Rechenbach, Jeffrey	CWA	1994–present
Richardson, Robert E.	Laborers	1996–present
Riger, Morris	Textile Workers	1958–1962
Rittenhouse, William	Retail Clerks	1974–1977
Robertson, Tom	UFCW	1994–1995 1995–present
Romine, Charles	Oil, Chemical & Atomic	1958–1960 1962–1964
Rose, William A.	USWA	1996–present
Ross, Ray	UAW	1958–1968
Royster, Wesley	GMP	1997–present
Rugola, Joseph	AFSCME/OAPSE	1988–present
Rusen, Paul D.	USWA	1958–1960 1962–1964 1982–1986
Ryan, Tom	CWA	1971–1972
Schremp, Paul	USWA	1958–1960 1962–1964 1966–1968
Schultz, William	IUE	1969–1970
Sedivy, Joseph	IBEW	1970–1983
Seibert, Henry	Clothing Workers	1958–1959
Sepate, Joseph	Clothing Workers	1962–1964
Serraglio, Nicholas	Allied Industrial Workers	1972–1974
Sheehan, William P.	Federal Labor	1974–1983

Ohio AFL-CIO Executive Board Members (continued)

Shields, Robert	Fire Fighters	1994–present
Shump, Joe	IUE	1966–1972
Smigel, Carl	Allied Industrial Workers	1962–1972
Snoots, William	IUE	1958–1960
Sowers, Larry	Carpenters	1995–present
Stamper, Wiley E.	IUE	1983–1989
Thorley, David	URW	1974–1976
Tucker, Donald	URW	1968–1974
Tucker, Arnold	IAM	1974–1978
Tutoki, Patricia A.	IUE	1981–1988
Valenta, Frank J.	USWA	1978–1994
Vickers, Franklin D.	USWA	1990–present
Vinegard, John	Hotel & Restaurant	1964–1974
Wagner, John D.	Plumbers & Pipefitters	1990–present
Walker, David	URW	1973–1974
Ward, Larry	Mine Workers	1994–1996
Watson, Geneva	AFSCME/OCSEA	1994–1995
Wemer, Gail	IUE	1974–1976
Wharton, Donald	IAM	1990–1995
White, Herschel	Hotel & Restaurant	1958–1964
Williams, David	Building Trades	1997–present
Williamson, B. G.	IBEW	1974–1988
Willis, Cenia	AFSCME	1994–present
Winslow, Dan	USWA	1995–present
Witte, Paul J.	IBEW	1988–present
Young, Robert	URW	1974–1982
Zalac, John P.	Boilermakers	1970–1974
Zannella Sr., Philip M.	IAM	1976–present
Zeuch, Edward	USWA	1972–1990

NOTE ON SOURCES

Historians have not written very extensively on recent Ohio history. George W. Knepper, *Ohio and Its People* (1998), is the most up-to-date survey of the state's past. Alexander P. Lomis, (ed.), *Ohio Politics: A Historical Perspective* (1994) contains valuable essays written by academics and journalists on various aspects of state government including the General Assembly, the Supreme Court, each of the Governors beginning with Frank Lausche in 1945. Raymond Boryczka and Lorin Lee Cary, *No Strength Without Union: An Illustrated History of Ohio Workers 1803-1980* (1982) is an excellent overview of the state's labor history, but does not deal extensively with the Ohio AFL-CIO. Rather, Raymond Boryczka addresses some of the Federation's activities in the pamphlet "United in Purpose: A Chronological History of the Ohio AFL-CIO, 1958-1983" (1985) available through The Ohio Historical Society. For a scholarly account of the 1958 right-to-work battle, see Glenn W. Miller and Stephan B. Ware, "Organized Labor in the Political Process: A Case Study of the Right-to-Work Campaign in Ohio," *Labor History* (Winter 1963), 51-67.

The Ohio AFL-CIO has been extremely diligent in turning over its records to the Ohio Historical Society for public use. The last transfer of material in the summer of 1997 updated the Society's holdings through the 1980s. The collection contains hundreds of boxes on an array of subjects and is a vital resource for anyone working on the political and economic history of the state. It is supplemented, moreover, by a number of private collections and oral histories obtained in the 1970s and 1980s by the

Historical Society as part of the Ohio Labor History Project. Among the more valuable records at the Society for this book were the papers of Elmer Cope, John Rooney, Ruth V. See, and the oral histories given by Jacob Clayman, Harry Mayfield, Ray Ross, and Pat O'Malley. The Historical Society's extensive collection of newspapers from around the state was also of critical importance.

The Ohio AFL-CIO also maintains a library at its headquarters that contains the most complete run of the organization's convention proceedings, minutes of Executive Board meetings, and various publications including *Focus* and *News and Views*. Also in the library are specialized materials dealing with workers' compensation, health and safety, political action, civil rights, women's issues, and other topics on which the organization has major interest.

INDEX